KISSING IN THE CHAPEL, PRAYING IN THE FRAT HOUSE

KISSING IN THE CHAPEL, PRAYING IN THE FRAT HOUSE

Wrestling with Faith and College

Edited by Adam J. Copeland

An Alban Institute Book

ROWMAN & LITTLEFIELD
Lanham • Boulder • New York • London

Published by Rowman & Littlefield
A wholly owned subsidiary of The Rowman & Littlefield Publishing Group,
Inc.
4501 Forbes Boulevard, Suite 200, Lanham, Maryland 20706
www.rowman.com

16 Carlisle Street, London W1D 3BT, United Kingdom

British Library Cataloguing in Publication Information Available

Library of Congress Cataloging-in-Publication Data
Kissing in the chapel, praying in the frat house / [edited by] Adam Copeland.
pages cm
ISBN 978-1-56699-765-2 (cloth : alk. paper) -- ISBN 978-1-56699-730-0 (pbk. : alk. paper) --
ISBN 978-1-56699-731-7 (electronic)
1. Young adults--Religious life. 2. Christian life. 3. Conduct of life. 4. Christianity and culture. I.
Copeland, Adam, 1983- editor.
BV4529.2.K5475 2014
248.8'34--dc23
2014028357

Printed in the United States of America

To M,
my college sweetheart

CONTENTS

SECTION III: SEX AND SEXUALITY: ONE BODY, MANY MEMBERS

SECTION IV: WALKING WITH OTHERS (OR, SOMETIMES, RUNNING FROM THEM)

SECTION V: STUDYING OFF-CAMPUS, STUDYING WITHIN

INTRODUCTION

Goodbye. I must have said "bye" to my parents hundreds of times before, but never had I done so with so much emotion (not counting a problematic separation anxiety stage in preschool). There we stood on the front lawn of my first college dormitory about to say our parting words. Within minutes my parents would be leaving, driving their rental car back to the airport to fly the fifteen hundred miles home. I would not be joining them. I was starting college.

What did my parents—what did I—imagine would take place over the next four years as they left their firstborn son in the care of college administrators they did not know, roommates they did not trust, and parties they did not sanction? What experiences would shake me to my core? What tears would I cry? What subjects would I study? What friends would I make? What decisions would I regret?

A few days after that goodbye, I attended Sunday morning worship on campus with several new friends from my dorm. At my small, liberal arts, church-related college, worship attendance wasn't quite expected, but it was certainly accepted. The overall culture of the college encouraged faith exploration, and the campus congregation was no exception. I did not know it then, but I would end up attending worship more often than not throughout my college career. Along with late-night pizza, gallons of coffee, and my fair share of cheap beer, Sunday worship and daily chapel services became part of my weekly college diet.

The student congregation, and the leadership of the college pastors, choirs, and organist, nourished my faith on Sunday mornings, but that hour functioned as one small piece of my larger college faith puzzle. I can name religion courses, off-campus study, creative writing courses, three choirs, conferences, classroom assignments, spring break trips, and dozens of relationships that were much more instrumental in my faith formation. But worship, nevertheless, marked many Sundays.

It is not coincidence that both the journey through college and the journey of Christian faith recognize formal stages of progress. In college, one begins as a freshman (or, increasingly, "first-year") often without a major and moves through the ranks of course credits, degree requirements, capstone experiences, and eventually a formal graduation. In many Christian churches, faith steps marked include baptism, receiving first Communion, confirmation, and eventually becoming a full adult member of a congregation. Death, sometimes called the "completion of baptism," eventually follows. In the winding journey of discovery, self-understanding, and formal stages, faith and college share a kinship. For many people, one cannot truly progress without the other.

The essays within the pages of *Kissing in the Chapel, Praying in the Frat House: Wrestling with Faith and College* speak to the many connections of faith and college. It is true that in most colleges and universities students can manage, if they wish, to leave their faith unexamined. In fact, some professors discourage all faith-related discussions in the classroom—talk of faith can get emotional after all, not to mention political. Even at private, faith-related schools, students can stoop to boilerplate answers or accurate scholarly analysis without examining their own faith claims. The writers in this collection, however, have refused to uphold the false dichotomy between faith and learning. Indeed, their reflections provide insight into how faith can deepen—and complicate—every aspect of one's college experience.

Commentators have already spilled much ink on the millennial generation, those born between 1980 and 2000, approximately. We're told today's twentysomethings, as well as those of us in our early thirties, are lazier than previous generations. We marry later, we are less likely to be affiliated with traditional religious beliefs, and more than a few move back into our parents' basements after college. While generational theory can be helpful for some big-picture, wide-ranging descriptions, it breaks down when it comes to individuals. That's where stories come in. Personal narratives can break through the broad brushstrokes of generational theory and describe real, unique, individual experiences in all their troubled beauty. This book came about because I was tired of hearing my generation described by outside "experts" in ways that sounded vaguely familiar, but lacked the passion and particularity of individual stories so important for true understanding.

To find the twenty-one fine contributors included in these pages, I took a multilayered approach to solicit submissions from around the nation (and world, as it turned out). Beginning the summer of 2012, I sought essays written by those in, or very near, their twenties. A call for submissions hosted on my personal website (adamjcopeland.com) was shared widely on social networks and garnered thousands of hits. Next, with the help of R. Austin Nelson, a fine student assistant to whom I'm most grateful, I contacted campus pastors, English and religion departments, and university faith networks to help identify gifted writers with a compelling faith and college story to tell. In all, I received more than fifty submissions from twentysomethings in the United States, Britain, and Canada. As the editing process continued, I commonly heard from the writers that they appreciated the process of writing and reflecting on their stories, regardless of whether or not their essay was selected for inclusion in the collection. The process of wrestling with faith and college, embracing the mystery and sharing the meaning, continues well beyond graduation.

The book is organized into five sections, though most of the essays could easily fit in more than one area. In some sense, they all deal with questions of identity, authority, and community, but each writer's story resists any attempts to be neatly organized into thematic categories. Indeed, the essays beg for conversation, so I have included Questions for Discussion at the end of each chapter.

In the first section, "(A)Tradition: Come, Ye Disconsolate" I include essays on students' experience with their expectations of the traditional on campus. Section II, "Who Am I? Who is God? What Am I to Do? Stories of Call," contains stories of the search for one's purpose and vocation. While essays throughout the book include some approaches to sexuality, the third section, "Sex and Sexuality: One Body, Many Members," includes essays that directly address questions of coming out, gender identity, and sexual mores. The next section, "Walking with Others (Or, Sometimes, Running from Them)," explores the notion that while wrestling with faith and college is often a communal activity, it is ultimately one that must be worked out for the individual. Finally, section V, "Studying Off-Campus, Studying Within," includes essays that expand the scope of campus life to summers, semesters abroad, and the inner city. Short introductions to each section serve to orient the reader to the particular type of college and faith experiences to follow.

My interest in the themes found in these pages is more than academic. Born in 1983 and thus a member of the millennial generation myself, the portrayal of millennials affects my own self-understanding and expression. More than once, I have presented on millennials, whether to a church group or within the academy, and while the descriptors leave my mouth, and graphs of generational expressions illumine the screen behind me, I have thought, "But . . . this isn't true for me . . . or my friend Tory, or my lunch buddy Andrew, or my college classmate Lindsey, or my seminary colleague Buz." As a millennial myself, the stories in these pages help give voice to those thoughts I have often not shared.

My approach to editing this collection also reflects my status as an ordained clergyperson in the Presbyterian Church (U.S.A.). As I worked through the essays with each writer, I reflected myself on how college can push, prod, and deepen religious convictions. While I myself align with a certain Christian tradition, my bias in editing this collection was to ensure the stories presented in these pages are faithful to each writer's authentic experience. My faith calls for a freedom to listen to diverse voices, even and especially ones that make me reexamine my convictions. In other words: no story has been censored out of theological concern.

Finally, my interest in these writers' stories flows also from my position as a member of the religion faculty at a small, church-related, liberal arts college. On the one hand, as a professor I have certain access to the lives of college students today. I see students every day and teach them several times a week in class. I read their essays, meet with them during office hours, and follow many of them on Twitter. On the other hand, while my position on a college faculty allows me more insight than the average person into the lives of college students, the process of editing this book has also made me acutely aware of the limits of my understanding. The stories in these pages have alerted me that there is a whole world of college students' experience to which faculty rarely gain access. Beyond access, however, I believe the follow-ing chapters will be valuable to college faculty and administrators be-cause, as the writers tell their stories, they also begin to make meaning from them. The chapters that follow are not simply action reports of what happened to students' faith in college, but also reflective, often beautiful, and sometimes heart-wrenching stories of wise young adults seeking to understand the world, God, and the powerful events that affect faith in college.

As a millennial pastor-turned-professor, some of the stories in these pages are difficult to read. A few make me nostalgic for my college days, while others describe university experiences very different from my own. It is my fervent hope that these pages will serve as a valuable resource both to those in higher education and to those in Christian ministry.

Four years after my parents and I said "goodbye" outside my first college dormitory, they made the trek back to campus for my gradua-tion. The commencement ceremony took place on a Sunday afternoon, preceded by a morning baccalaureate worship service. Because the crowd was too large for the college chapel, it took place in the gym filled to the brim with soon-to-be graduates, family, and friends. Though I was thrilled to be graduating, I felt a strong sense of loss on that late spring day. Caught up in the day's emotions, I believed that the richness of my college experience could not be duplicated later in life. So, while I was more than happy to be granted a diploma, I was not ready to "commence." I was not eager for college to end as those four years, cliché or not, had actually been the best four years of my life. Then, it was with a heart already filled to the brim that I began singing the closing hymn.

> Go my children, with my blessing, never alone;
> Waking, sleeping, I am with you, you are my own,
> In my love's baptismal river I have made you mine forever,
> Go, my children, with my blessing, You are my own. [1]

The hymn text of Jaroslav Vajda (about whom I had written a semi-nar paper) stung with significance. I was aware that the hymn had been

---

1.   Text by Jaroslav J. Vajda © 1983 Concordia Publishing House, cph.org. Used by per-mission. All rights reserved.

criticized for putting words in God's mouth, but for me that graduation morning, the words felt heaven-sent.

> Go, my children, sins forgiven, at peace and pure,
> Here you learned how much I love you, what I can cure;
> Here you heard my Son's dear story,
> Here you touched him, saw his glory,
> Go, my children, sins forgiven, at peace and pure.

I had to silently mouth the next verse, tears in my eyes. Surrounded by a college community and a faith community that had given me books to read, papers to write, songs to sing, and friends to love, I knew those words were more true than I could ever have known four years prior. On that college campus, I *had* learned how much God loved me. And, at points along my college journey, I had touched and been touched by God's glory. Through God's grace, my many college sins had been forgiven.

Eyes glistening with tears, yet thankful for my college years, I rallied to sing the final verse. They were words I had heard a dozen times, but with that congregation, with that graduating class, in that place, in the closing moments of baccalaureate, the meaning soared beyond any I had known before.

> Go, my children, fed and nourished, closer to me.
> Grow in love and love by serving, joyful and free.
> Here my Spirit's power filled you;
> Here my tender comfort stilled you.
> Go, my children, fed and nourished, joyful and free.

My experience of wrestling with faith and college laid the foundation for a future in graduate school, pastoral service, and, eventually, a return to the academy. The writers included in this collection are working in nonprofits, starting new churches, leading efforts toward interfaith cooperation, studying for graduate degrees, and more. They wrestled mightily with faith and college. Now, as they share their stories, it's our turn to do the same.

Adam J. Copeland
Lent 2014

Section I

(A)Tradition:
Come, Ye Disconsolate

For many students, college is a time to test the beliefs and values of their upbringing. Away from home for the first time, they encounter new ideas, diverse people, and exciting freedoms. The challenges can be immense—how to negotiate life with a roommate, whether to wake up and go to church hungover, where to find quarters for the dorm washing machine—and over the course of four short years, previous understandings shift significantly. The four essays in this section all deal with these difficult questions as students face what of their faith should remain constant, and what must change.

In "Let the Whole Creation Cry: On Learning Hymns," Taylor Brorby tells of his hesitancy to face a required religion course and his eventual embrace of faith and hymns. While Brorby's essay is set in a small Minnesota college campus, Mary Ellen Jebbia's piece, "We Are All Prophets," considers her California campus with more than ten times as many students as Brorby's. Jebbia's Catholic upbringing sets the context for an embrace of interfaith advocacy and a reconsideration of her own faith. The third essay considers campus life at one of the country's leading Bible colleges, Moody Bible Institute, where Brandan Robertson matriculated after years of anticipation. In "How Bible College Caused Me to Lose My Faith (and Find It Again)" Robertson shares his fascinating journey of struggle and eventual acceptance. Finally, Kristi

Del Vecchio's essay, "After Prayerful Consideration: Becoming a Religious Atheist" brings the reader back to Minnesota—and India—as she claims her voice as a secular student at a church-related college, even as she embraces the academic study of religion and her role in the interfaith movement. In sum, each essay considers tradition as the writers reach beyond some, delve deeper into others, and claim their own.

I

LET THE WHOLE CREATION CRY

On Learning Hymns

Taylor Brorby

In my youth, I hated hymns. Monotonous, stuffy, and ancient, hymns reminded me of an attic. The hymns I knew seemed as outdated as the church itself, and I was content to keep their oppressive language, like the attic, out of sight, and out of mind. Growing up, my family did not attend church regularly, earning us the cheeky "Chreaster" Christians, a wonderful mash-up of words describing those who only attend church on Christmas and Easter.

In high school I was fervently antireligious. To me, it didn't add up: How could people believe in a God, especially a three-in-one God? More ridiculous: How could a person walk on water? Even more: A virgin birth?! Poppycock. But my contempt for religious insensibility was solely sequestered to Christianity. Hinduism, Judaism, Buddhism, the ancient religions of Mediterranean Egypt, Macedonia, Greece, and Rome were excused. They were not the faiths of the community I came from, they were not a part of my upbringing, and, to my young mind, I did not have to grapple with their complexities.

For better or worse—I thought worse—I attended a liberal arts college in southeastern Minnesota. Placed upon a hill, St. Olaf College outwardly appealed to my aesthetic: limestone buildings met with winsome Norwegian maples. What in its design wasn't to love?

Religion class.

I was hesitant to attend a religiously affiliated school. And St. Olaf College not only required a first-year Bible class, but another in theology, as well as an ethics course. I felt that this was indoctrination. I thought the study of religion had no place in education.

My first class was an 8:00 a.m. class about anthropology and the Bible. I was not going to buy this gray-haired man's arguments; I was definitely against the Word of God. (I did not understand the first rule of criticism meant you actually needed to read a book to have an opinion about it.)

Our class was held in the basement of the college chapel, which reminded me of those stuffy, old hymns. The room was spartan: a few desks, a blackboard, and white walls enclosing the room. It felt like a cell.

My professor, a man gray about the temples, had theological degrees from both a seminary and a theological school in Germany. Perhaps his most infectious phrase, one that I kept wrestling with over the semester, was his clause after he said the word God. "God, if there is a god . . . ." My professor opened room for doubt. In hindsight, I came to eventually understand that the preaching of religion was different from the teaching of religion.

I still wasn't convinced. The Religious Life was for those nut-jobs that gave their life over to the Spirit, or Jesus, or God, who, in the words of the writer and atheist Christopher Hitchens, was capable of convicting you of thoughtcrime, a type of celestial North Korea. That sounded about right to me. Who would want a God who "has a plan," as so many people purport? Or, more frighteningly, who wants a God that watches you waking and sleeping? That's spooky, not godly.

After a suggestion from a friend, I rolled into a pew for daily chapel. (Attending church on Sunday was too tall an order yet.) I found it odd. Daily chapel was a time that created space for song, for silence, for rich words and language to buzz in my ears. It was a time for me to take a break from the demands of academe and myself, and it allowed me to reorient my compass to what was most important to me: time spent in community.

In high school, making music was more who I was than what I did. My schedule was filled with wind ensemble, jazz band, music theory, and leading sectionals. I spent my time outside of school practicing, attending recitals, playing in the orchestra, taking piano lessons, and enjoying conducting lessons with the local orchestra maestro. I wanted to pull sound from metal and wood, to stand on a podium and be washed with rich harmonies. I longed for beauty to be a part of my daily life.

Instead, my piano teacher crushed me with mechanized exercises by Czerny, Burgmüller, and Hanon. I played Bach to my chagrin, finding him difficult and rigid. I loved Beethoven, adored Brahms, and embraced Schubert. But my teacher wanted me to get creative. She wanted me to improvise, and that meant opening a hymnal.

In college my eventual daily chapel attendance grew to include Sunday worship with the student congregation. Larger, more ceremonial, filled with music by choirs, brass and bell ensembles, soloists, and chant, Sunday mornings at St. Olaf taught me an important Lutheran college adage: no matter how late you were out partying, get up in time to get to church.

It was not so much a belief in a divine creator that sent me on my way to church, but the music and the community. Like my piano lessons, I kept opening a hymnal, finding familiar melodies like "Ein feste Burg" and "Wachet auf, ruft uns die Stimme." (The humble church of my childhood did not have a choir; it did not even have an organ. It had a pastor and piano player.)

Boe Memorial Chapel, an immense A-framed building on the college campus, is an imposing structure, replete with stained glass, a large organ, two pastors, flags representing students from around the world, a blue ceiling, and tiled floors. It is a sensory delight for a discerning eye.

Eventually, I came to consider Boe my home. I would visit it during its quiet times and play piano, riffing on my favorite hymns, during twilight. I felt like I resided in Boe and Boe in me.

Boe did not only host daily chapel and my excursions in piano playing. I would often slide into a pew while a friend was playing a Widor organ prelude, or enjoy the shaking of the stained glass during Saint-Saens's immense Organ Symphony. Boe held the arts, playing host to the college bands, choirs, and orchestras. Boe supported my college community.

But this was odd. When did the shift in my religious sensibility occur? When did I embrace the church? There is no moment I can point to. No moment where I walked to a window in my underwear, looking at the moonlight pouring through my windowpane, jolting when The Voice of God said, "Taylor, you must attend church!"

What happened in college was immense change. I studied widely, taking courses in sociology, English, Norwegian, mathematics, religion, philosophy, and American studies. I came to see the human narrative as a long arc in my history classes, one that was infused with perennial questions, such as "What does it mean to be human?" "How do we best live in place?" "What is the origin of the universe?"

I did not start attending church hoping to find answers to these questions. I wanted, as Rainer Maria Rilke says, to live the questions. These questions provided me rich food in college: they fed me deeply and cooked up great conversation between friends.

I came to believe that chapel and Sunday church attendance were my time creating beauty. I would listen to stories of struggle, of addiction, of mission, of vocation—stories infused by the lives of real people whom I knew and loved.

But those hymns.

I came to view them differently. The Danish philosopher Søren Kierkegaard said that in the simple is the eternal, and I found myself bumbling across campus, humming the tunes of "Beautiful Savior," "Let the Whole Creation Cry," and "How Can I Keep from Singing?" Something snagged me.

Maybe it was the knowledge that F. Melius Christiansen did something remarkable at my college, that he started a now long-standing tradition of a cappella singing.

No, that wasn't it. That story wasn't that interesting to me.

What was interesting to me was the story of his son, Paul, who eventually went on to teach at Concordia College in Moorhead, Minnesota. Paul was known as a roustabout, a consummate musician even in high school, and a party animal. Some nights Paul would not come home until the early morning hours, at which point he would start playing hymns. In the early part of the last century it was customary to play the four-to-one chord progression after a hymn, the typical "Amen" ending. Paul, at the end of his playing, would tromp up to bed, leaving the hymn incomplete. He didn't play the "Amen." His father, F. Melius, scurried down the stairs to play the Amen, then he returned to bed for the night.

This was the story I loved; this story showed the human side of faith, it showed the richness of life. It is a story that shows that deep beauty, deep conviction, deep faith is not always a public display, that it can also live in our private moments. It was a story I embraced—and still do—finding myself both laughing and smiling when I retell it. Laughing because it is amusing to think of a father being unable to sleep due to an unfinished hymn, and smiling because, to me, it shows the still-growing faith of a young man.

Like Paul, I too play hymns after a late night. But what grabbed me? Was it solely the melodies? What I eventually discovered was that the language of the hymn writers resonated deeply with me, it washed over me and left me feeling supported.

As a young man I grew up among prairies and pastures, rivers and buttes, lakes and lazy summer afternoons. I was free to wander and explore the natural world beyond my back yard. It makes sense that the first hymn I committed to memory was Folliott Sandford Pierpoint's "For the Beauty of the Earth," with such wonderful language as this:

> For the beauty of each hour of the day and of the night,
> hill and vale, and tree and flower, sun and moon, and stars of light;
> Christ, our Lord, to thee we raise this our sacrifice of praise.

Or Timothy Dudley-Smith's "As One Unknown," (whose tune I learned in my piano lessons as "Dear Lord and Father of Mankind"):

> He comes to us in sound of seas,
> the ocean's fume and foam;
> yet small and still upon the breeze,
> a wind that stirs the tops of trees,
> a voice to call us home,
> a voice to call us home.

I loved that language—fume, foam, vale—the idea that the earth could infuse a language that made me feel both comfortable and expansive. I needed that language. I still need that language.

Perhaps the hymn I needed most in college was #607 in the *Evangelical Lutheran Worship* hymnal, "Come, Ye Disconsolate." I discovered this hymn when I learned my maternal grandmother's appendix burst and she made the decision not to have an operation. (She walked around with her burst appendix for two days before going to the hospital. There, the doctors told her that if she had the operation she would be relegated to a nursing home or that, during surgery, she might die. Electing not to have the surgery my grandma chose to die on her own terms. She then told her family stories, told us she loved us. Her last meal was a banana-flavored popsicle, and then my grandmother died.)

"Come, Ye Disconsolate" is rich, using language that evokes the King James Bible, and suffused with a gentle melody. It was what I needed at that moment contemplating my grandmother's death, it's what I would later need during finals, and it was what supported me when my parents found out I was gay. Here is the language I so desperately love:

> Come, ye disconsolate, where'er ye languish;
> come to the mercy seat, fervently kneel.
> Here bring your wounded hearts, here tell your anguish;
> earth has no sorrow that heav'n cannot heal.
>
> Joy of the desolate, light of the straying,
> hope of the penitent, fadeless and pure;
> here speaks the Comforter, tenderly saying,
> "Earth has no sorrow that heav'n cannot cure."
>
> Here see the Bread of life, see waters flowing
> forth from the throne of God, pure from above.
> Come to the feast of love; come, ever knowing
> earth has no sorrow but heav'n can remove. [1]

I still play hymns, a practice I came to fully embrace in college. I greet the morning with a song, usually "Awake, My Soul, and with the Sun," and end my night with a well-known tune, like "All Praise to Thee, My God, This Night." These songs are now the bookends to my day, and they let me contemplate something beautiful in the morning and calm me before a night of rest. The hymns of my childhood are no longer monotonous, stuffy, and ancient. They are a cloak that I use to wrap myself each day.

---

1. Thomas Moore, stanza 1–2; Thomas Hastings, stanza 3, "Come, Ye Disconsolate," in *Evangelical Lutheran Worship* (Minneapolis: Augsburg Fortress, 2006), http://www. hymnary.org/hymn/ELW2006/607.

QUESTIONS FOR DISCUSSION

1. What impact have hymns and songs had in your experience of faith and life?
2. Brorby's religion professor used the phrase "God, if there is a god . . . ," which complicates Brorby's preconceptions about college religion classes. Should such a strategy be employed consistently by religion professors?
3. Boe Memorial Chapel became a sort of home for Brorby. What can colleges and universities do to support the creation and sustaining of sacred space on campus?

2

WE ARE ALL PROPHETS

Mary Ellen Jebbia

One morning when I was in second grade, we received a simple assignment. The assignment seemed simple, at least: draw yourself as a grown-up. My classmates began to draw themselves as doctors, professional basketball players, artists, and veterinarians. I thought about how to draw me performing my dream job. After a few minutes, I shrugged, and began to draw my future self. My teacher paced around the classroom slowly, smiling and encouraging the other students. When she reached my desk she stopped and looked confused.

"What are you doing in this picture, Mary Ellen?"

I felt ashamed. Was my dream job silly? I looked up at my teacher, trying not to make eye contact. "It's me parting the Red Sea, like Moses," I mumbled.

"Oh," my teacher murmured, still confused. "Then . . . what is your dream job?"

Now everyone was looking at me. I felt hot and uncomfortable. Why couldn't I have just drawn myself as a scientist? I couldn't lie now, so instead just blurted out, "I want to be one of God's prophets, like Moses."

The other students stared at me with utter confusion, probably thinking, "That's not a job! Why would God make you one of His prophets? What makes you so special?"

The same questions plagued me. I didn't know God would be convinced that I could be brave or worthy like the prophets we read about in our picture Bibles. I just knew that I wanted to be God's servant, because I loved God and Jesus. Perhaps this was too much for a seven year old to really understand.

In second grade at my Catholic elementary school, we received two sacraments. The first was our First Reconciliation, in which we confessed our sins to a priest in private, and he assigned us prayers to say to ask for God's forgiveness. The second sacrament was our First Communion, which would be the first time we were allowed to receive the Eucharist at mass. I distinctly remember my father telling me that the day I received my First Communion was "more important than my birthday."

We spent much of our time at school practicing the order of the mass for the ceremony: how to enter, exit, sing the hymns, recite the prayers—and of course, how to receive the bread and eat it. I remember my teacher harshly chastising the boy next to me for spitting the Eucharist out because he despised the taste. I practiced my prayers at home, in the car on the way to and from school, and before bed. I wanted to be perfect, to show God I cared more than anything about this. I wanted God to be proud of me, and hopefully someday, to trust me with His messages and to carry out His plan for us, His children.

Unlike many of my peers growing up, I never "left" the church. The church never hurt me, or caused me to feel unhappy or lost. The year after I received my First Communion, I joined my best friend's all Japanese-American travel basketball team. We practiced every weekend at a Japanese community center in Southern California. I never imagined being different from my teammates, not just in ethnicity but in every aspect of our identities. It never occurred to me that my teammates might not understand my love for God and my devotion to my religion. Some of my teammates did not believe in God; their families were Buddhist.

One day after practice my teammates had begun a game of hide and seek, and as the seeker, I sprinted around the community center, interrupting Japanese language and cooking classes, trying to find the hiders. At one point, I pulled the door of the small community Buddhist temple wide open without thinking, and froze. People were praying toward brass deities on an altar, with incense wafting through the air, and they were bowing and mumbling. What kind of church was this? Was this my teammates' way of praying to God?

As it had never occurred to me that different religions existed, it also never occurred to me that others were wrong or bad. My teammates and I were the same, right? So their way of praying must simply be different. No one taught me to hate or fear, so I didn't. In school we learned that God loved all His children. Perhaps God gave us different ways to pray, because we were all unique.

As time passed, I began to realize others did not see me as Japanese. I wanted so much to prove my Japanese identity. Spending so much time with my basketball team, I wanted to prove my likeness to them in every way. I began to study Japanese outside of school with a tutor, and begged my father to take me to Japan. In seventh grade, I applied to boarding schools (much to the chagrin of my mother and father) that would allow me to study in Japan. I did end up studying in Japan my junior year of high school. At that point, I had already become keenly interested in religions, as my boarding school attracted students from all over the world and thus of many different faith traditions. One might expect with my religious upbringing that I would scorn these other faiths in order to show my faith was the only right way. But the truth is, no one had ever actually taught me that my faith was "right" and that I should consider other religions to be false.

While studying in Japan, I took the crowded Sobu-sen train line to school every morning, passing through Japan's most crowded train station, Shinjuku. Once or twice a week, I liked to walk through Shinjuku above the train station on the way home from school because the colors and lights fascinated me. The station shops and restaurants outside sat beneath skyscrapers with advertisements pieced together like a Tetris game. One easily felt overwhelmed by the bustle and noise. One day, I noticed a small Buddhist temple sat humbly off one of the side streets. I decided to go in.

The entrance to the temple was a simple yet stunning garden with a path leading to the building. As I stepped onto the property, my body experienced an immediate sense of tranquility. It was striking how different I felt only two steps away from the noisy streets. Suddenly I forgot all the stress of the urban metropolis outside, and felt only a sense of calm. A few people strolled around the garden, taking their time, seeming to feel the same peace and ease, unbothered by the outside distractions.

Inside the temple a simple altar with a statue of Buddha holding his hands with one palm facing up and one facing out sat in the middle. The smell of incense hung in the air and the room flickered with dimly lit candles. I observed people kneeling on one of the many pillows scattered around the room, sitting motionless, with their eyes closed. I did the same. Thoughts began to float through my head and finally they stopped. When I opened my eyes, I felt a sense of belonging, something right. I visited that temple every week for the rest of my time in Japan. During my senior year of high school, I began to study Buddhism, and found that the way I experienced God began to change.

My parents have always supported me in my interests and endeavors. As owners of small businesses, they understand that trying new things might be scary, but is the only way to be a successful leader. Starting college, my father strongly encouraged me to study business along with my other interests. I was fortunate to attend the University of Southern California's Marshall School of Business. I enjoyed business because of its emphasis on relationship building and ethics, but studying business didn't fill my soul. I knew Japanese and religion were my real passions. I decided to triple major, and minor in International Relations, just to round things out. This course would require an extra year of study and an extra class each semester, but my parents approved, so I persevered. I loved my classes and professors. The readings provoked so many questions for me. When we took occasional field trips to houses of worship I marveled at the beauty of each. The academic in me felt quite satisfied. Yet, something was still missing.

Now, as a recent college graduate, I have realized that religion is a living, breathing practice. Texts and writings provide a baseline for our understanding of theology and belief patterns, but the real heart of religion and spirituality lies in the people who claim and practice these traditions. What was missing my first two years of college was a chance for me to experience this in my life. As a practicing Buddhist who still attended Catholic Mass on a semiregular basis, I found that while I loved my faith and the questions it raised, I also felt confused, scared, and alone at times, just as many of us do. I needed an outlet to share these feelings. My opportunity came as a complete fluke.

I worked as an assistant in the Global Business Programs office. One day, sitting bored at my desk, I pulled the *Daily Trojan*, our student run newspaper, out of the recycling bin. One of the headlines read "New

Dean of Religious Life to start at USC July 1st." I didn't even know USC had a Dean of Religious Life, much less an Office of Religious Life. As it turned out, the new Dean would be the first Hindu in this position at any university in the country.

Dean Varun Soni boasted quite an interesting life so far. He had studied in Nepal and India as a Buddhist monk, graduated from Harvard Divinity School and UCLA Law School, hosted a radio show, and even started a graphic novel company. He sounded just like me, or rather, the person I wanted to be—someone whose passion was religion, yet who could take this passion in numerous directions.

All this time I felt confused about which path I could take, and it turns out, as Dean Soni demonstrated, I could take them all. People used to ask me, "What on earth will you do with religion and business? Those don't go together." I answer with a teaching of the Buddha: Everything in this world is interconnected. Sometimes you just have to draw the lines yourself. What won't I do?

I e-mailed Dean Soni, asking to meet with him when he arrived on campus. I felt nervous and excited—what was I going to say? Five minutes into the meeting, though, I knew pulling that newspaper out of the bin was fate. Dean Soni opened my eyes to a whole world on campus about which I had no idea. USC boasts the most international student body of any university in the United States, as well as over ninety student religious and spiritual organizations. Over sixty houses of worship sit within walking distance of campus. How had I not known about this microcosm of spiritual life? Dean Soni suggested, besides exploring all these new opportunities, that I join the Interfaith Council, a group of students who met for dinner once a week to talk about questions of religion and spirituality, and occasionally perform service projects. I gladly accepted, and remarked at how much my life had changed after that short meeting.

The Interfaith Council quickly became my family on campus. The students that attended meetings excelled in many different fields—both in the classroom and in their leadership outside the classroom. I found myself hanging on every word of every dialogue. The questions students asked, the doubts they felt, as well as the reinforcement of their faith through this interaction, helped me understand my own faith journey more clearly. I was not considered strange for feeling connected to two very different faith traditions. I finally felt like my course of study meant something to my entire identity as a student, a believer, and a human being.

A year after joining the council, I embarked on a yearlong fellowship around the world as part of a joint program of the Interfaith Youth Core in Chicago, Illinois, and the Tony Blair Faith Foundation in London, England. During the fellowship I taught and advocated for the UN Millennium Development Goals and the importance for people of faith to rally around these goals. I got the unbelievable privilege to study and work in London, Malawi, Chicago, and Boston, but even more importantly, I formed a substantial number of meaningful relationships that to this day help me remember how important my faith is to me. I came back to USC ready to lead the Interfaith Council and make our presence known on campus.

My biggest regret in college is not finding the Office of Religious Life and the Interfaith Council sooner. As a veteran of the council, I wanted to make sure we found those students who were searching for their family on campus. Now, completing a Master of Divinity at the University of Chicago Divinity School, I can fully attribute my life's path and the myriad of opportunities in front of me to that group of students and the Office of Religious Life that never ceased to support me as a student, an activist, and most importantly, a person of faith.

My experience in college mirrors that of many college students. College is a place for young people to take risks and challenge themselves, not just in the classroom, but also in all aspects of their life. As a student I saw many of my peers turn away from religion and faith because it wasn't considered "cool" or "scholarly"; perhaps some even consider it backward. I maintain, however, that all students need outlets to express themselves as young human beings apart from their studies. This may not be a religious experience for some, but as Dean Soni stated in his inauguration speech, "Every student needs a time and a place to reflect on their identity and purpose in this world." College is the time to learn this practice well. Students who do so will carry the practice with them in all their endeavors and, likely, will become strong leaders because they know themselves.

While the academic study of religion is important during college, interaction with people from different religions, spiritual traditions, and even of nonfaith backgrounds is just as crucial to the college experience. Such interactions help students open their minds and hearts, suggesting that their own search for identity and purpose is a lifelong venture. My favorite passage from the Holy Qur'an, from the Sura Al-Hujurat, states this best: "O mankind, indeed We have created you from male and female and made you peoples and tribes that you may know one another. Indeed, the most noble of you in the sight of Allah is the most righteous of you. Indeed, Allah is Knowing and Acquainted" (Qur'an 49:13).

While some colleges and universities around the country have taken enormous steps forward to promote religious and spiritual life on campus, we still have much work to do. I remember sitting at my kitchen table watching the news during Thanksgiving break of 2008, gawking in horror at the terrorist attacks that had hit the Taj Hotel in Mumbai. The Office of Religious Life held a candlelit service the next week, and many students, faculty, and staff came together to pray and reflect. Many of the students were South Asian, and many had direct familial connections to the attacks. At the end of the service, as people were directed to proceed to the sides of the church to light candles, I saw a student rush to the podium, attempting to grab the microphone. My first thought was that the student had lost a family member, and thus wanted to speak his grievances. I observed as Dean Soni took the microphone, trying to calm the student. The student began to look frustrated and angry. He stormed out. I learned later that this student wanted to spout hateful words about Pakistani people and their majority religion, Islam. Even after both Indian and Pakistani students stood together in prayer and hope minutes before, this wasn't enough to bridge the divide. These tensions, like religion and faith themselves, are living, breathing, powerful forces.

As young people of faith and belief, we need to stand up for peace on our campuses, and create space for dialogue around these tensions. If we cannot create these spaces at universities, the ultimate places for learning and exploration, how will we, as future leaders, know to create these spaces elsewhere? Just as Dean Soni noted that we must learn to find outlets for reflection in college, we also must promote space for dialogue and interaction with those holding different belief systems. The two go hand-in-hand.

Perhaps my seven-year-old self was not completely crazy. I may never be a prophet in the way Abraham or Moses were, but I can still carry out the work I believe to be "of God," that is, for me, working toward religious cooperation as a social norm in the world. A prophet strives to deliver messages to the wider world, and moreover to lead by example. In my work as an interfaith activist today, I spread the message of many traditions: that through our diversity as individuals but consistency in our values, we must aim to combat bigotry and hate. The best way to do this is to lead by example, by doing good in the world side-by-side with my friends of all faiths. As a child, no one taught me to hate, so I lived with a curious, open heart—just as all students should. We are all prophets in some way, we all have both messages to share and to hear.

QUESTIONS FOR DISCUSSION:

1. Jebbia writes that, "texts and writings provide a baseline for our understanding of theology and belief patterns, but the real heart of religion and spirituality lies in the people who claim and practice these traditions." Do you agree? How should college study balance religious texts and interactions with those who practice religions?

2. Dean Soni stated in his inauguration speech that all students need, "a time and a place to reflect on their identity and purpose in this world." Is this true? Where are the ideal times and spaces for such reflection?

3. At the colleges and universities you know, what is the status of interfaith cooperation?

3

HOW BIBLE COLLEGE CAUSED ME TO LOSE MY FAITH (AND FIND IT AGAIN)

Brandan Robertson

BIBLE COLLEGE: A DREAM COME TRUE

Growing up, there was nothing I looked forward to more than going to college. In my case, that meant Bible College. Ever since I became a Christian at the age of twelve, I knew that I was called to be a pastor, and I knew that meant that I needed to get a solid theological education. And so, nearly seven years in advance, I began exploring the hundreds of Christian colleges and universities in the United States to find which one would be the perfect fit. By the time I was seventeen and ready to apply, I had narrowed my preferences to one school, the Moody Bible Institute in Chicago. So finally receiving my acceptance letter was nothing short of a life transforming moment. My childhood dream was becoming a *reality*.

I came to Moody with very high expectations. I believed that Bible College was going to be *the* transformative experience of my life, changing me from a teenager to a pastor in just four short years. I expected to have an expedited sanctification process and to be practically sinless by my senior year. I know these expectations may seem laughable, but the truth is that *most* people who are bound for Bible College have similar hopes, though perhaps phrased in more palatable ways. This is due, in part, to the dramatic marketing that every college uses to sell itself as the *best place ever*. Moody rightly promotes its high-flying, church-planting graduates and also points to several very well-known evangelical leaders serving on its board. My own pastor in Maryland started his congregation right after graduating from Moody and it now averages over four thousand people attending every Sunday. Many new students learning about success stories like these often assume that it was Bible College that made these men and women into the big hitters they have become. In other words, I pretty much expected to be a megachurch pastor who would be numbered among the spiritual elite by the time I walked across the platform at graduation. Unrealistic? You bet. But, those were my expectations.

BURNT OUT ON BIBLE STUDY

My time at Moody began with a retreat to Lake Geneva in Wisconsin with the Moody Men's Choir. As the group roasted marshmallows and told stories around the bonfire, the upperclassmen began offering advice to us incoming freshmen. One piece of advice echoed again and again: "Guys, whatever you do, *don't* let the Bible become a textbook." Each of them went on to explain that in our years in Bible College we can begin to view our spiritual lives as part of our coursework and lose personal connection to God through things like Bible study and prayer. They explained that in various seasons of their college experience, they found themselves spiritually dry and disconnected. But, they said, it didn't have to be that way for us. Of course, we all listened attentively to these brothers' wisdom and took their admonitions very seriously. All of us, after all, were beginning the first stage of entering Christian ministry. What could be worse than becoming *disconnected from God* in the process?

It took about a week of class for me to realize exactly what the upperclassmen were talking about. Everywhere I went, everyone I talked to, it was all Bible all the time. In class we read the Bible, for homework I was required to study the Bible, and in my freshman zeal I was a part of a dozen Bible study groups. I also went to church every Sunday where we, well, read and were taught from the Bible. I served in an afterschool program teaching kids about God and the Bible. On top of all that, I was expected to read the Bible "devotionally" every day (as is customary for evangelicals) while maintaining a vibrant prayer life. Very quickly my faith began to be smothered. I had never thought it possible, but I found myself feeling like everything at Moody was *too* Christian. My faith was beginning to feel nothing more than a cultural artifact of this strange community of Bible College.

TRAPPED INSIDE THE BUBBLE

Over the course of my freshman year, I was transformed from being "Preacher Boy" (the nickname I earned in high school because of over-zealousness for my faith) to a jaded cynic. It turned out that this experience wasn't unique to me. In fact, one professor described our school as an "evangelical monastery" where for four years we leave the luxury of our "real" lives to go away and live in a community centered on our faith for a time of intense study and self-discipline. The problem was that this was not what I thought I had signed up for.

I had envisioned a pretty "typical" college experience—living in dorms, going out in the city, being challenged theologically and ideolog-ically, having fun, and of course sharpening my faith for Christian ser-vice. And in one sense, that *is* exactly what my college offered to me. But, the environment proved to be toxic for the health of my faith. I felt like the main character in the *The Truman Show*—trapped. Most stu-dents at Christian colleges have little access to television and media which means we know very little about current events. Even though most of us are active on social media, our connection and understanding of pop culture and the rest of the world around us begins to wane.

Due to the theological and faith requirements for admission to most Bible colleges, students are like-minded in our belief systems. This leads us to become closed-off with very little diversity or discussion with people of differing perspectives. Everyone generally believes the same things, has the same opinions, listens to the same music, reads the same books, and goes to the same churches. Not only does this become an incredibly boring utopian existence, but it is also simply impossible to grow in an environment like this. It's an environment where no one *really* thinks, but rather just affirms whatever their favorite professors affirm. If faith requires believing in that which isn't readily seen, such a college environment hinders faith because there God is *everywhere*. And not in the comforting sense of "the Lord is always with you" but rather in the incredibly annoying sense that *everything* becomes a spiritual matter and *every* minute detail of your life becomes a matter of faith.

CYNICISM

When this cynicism began to set in, I tried hard to combat it. I spent hours praying in a utility closet on our floor that had been christened the "prayer room." I read some pretty heavy Puritan writings on sin and became convinced that I was "hardening my heart" and wandering down the "slippery slope" that could eventually lead me to abandon my faith. This growing fear caused an enormous amount of anxiety for me. While I spent hours trying to pray and read the Bible, my desire to do so dwindled. I tried everything—from attending prayer meetings in our floor lounge at the crack of dawn to holding Bible studies in my room a couple nights a week. But as time went on, I decided to sleep-in or go out with my friends rather than attend my own Bible study. This was *not* a good sign!

When summer break finally came, I returned home to Maryland. Slowly but surely my faith began to return because outside of the "monastery" I was connected to the *real* world and hung out with *real* people who didn't believe the same things I did. I began reading my Bible and actually feeling nourished by it. I prayed and felt like God heard me. It felt like I had become a Christian all over again.

That is, until my sophomore year started. I arrived back on campus with a reinvigorated faith, but soon reverted back to cynicism because I felt, once again, that I could never get away from "God" (the *subject* not the Spirit!). But this year was different. Because I knew what to expect, I began to explore new ways to keep my faith alive. The first order of business was to find a church community that had no Moody students and was distinctly different than everything I was experiencing each day at school.

A couple of friends and I decided that we were going to go church shopping—visiting various denominations and traditions that we had never been exposed to. We went really exotic visiting Catholic, Eastern Orthodox, Lutheran, Presbyterian, Pentecostal, and *even* a Mormon church! Every week we experienced something fresh. Something compelling. Something *very different* than our day-to-day experience of faith at Moody. However, when we attended these new communities, we stuck out like sore thumbs. I once visited a progressive evangelical church with my friend just down the street from Moody. As soon as the service ended, one of the pastors approached us and said, "You're from Moody, *right?*" Of course! We were both college-aged and decked out in suits and ties, "proper" evangelical churchgoing attire.

As we visited more communities, we desperately tried to discover how *not* to look like "Moodies"—without much success. But nonetheless, these new experiences gave us renewed energy and helped combat our cynicism. Even though each Sunday we would return to campus to continue our work of studying the Bible, being taught evangelical theology, and attending chapel three times a week, we also brought back with us a broadened perspective and fresh experience.

We were learning things that none of us had ever encountered before. We began to feel like we were exotic. We were unique. We were the rebels. Who would have thought that simply visiting different churches would be one of the keys to surviving college? For me, it truly was. But as I began flirting with new ideas and perspectives I began to be considered an outsider and troublemaker by some in my community.

MAKING TROUBLE INSIDE THE BUBBLE

Within the first few months of school, two seemingly small events changed my life trajectory. First, my friends and I started a radio show on our campus student radio station. We named our show "The Bridge," inspired by our desire to bridge the divides between our faith tradition and the traditions we experienced on our Sunday visits to different churches in Chicago. The concept for the show included interviewing religious leaders from various backgrounds about the controversial issues surrounding their tradition to see if we could find some middle ground for agreement.

Our first show began by interviewing pastors of small, local congregations but very quickly opportunities began to open up for us to interview internationally known religious leaders from backgrounds and perspectives *very* different from our own. We jumped at the opportunity to interview these "celebrity" pastors, but as soon as we did we began to encounter pushback from other students and professors. One of the biggest dangers of being a closed community is that you can easily build walls so high that anything or anyone that tries to enter and that doesn't look, act, or think like you, cannot enter. We began interviewing people who many in our community considered "out there," and while a small group of students emerged that loved hearing the fresh insights and perspectives of our guests, many fellow students responded negatively. They argued that since it was *our school's* radio station, it should represent *our school's* perspective. When we began inviting people onto the show who didn't agree with the views of our institution, it was treated as if we were inviting an enemy into our camp.

This "one perspective mindset" is a posture that many faith-based institutions take and as harsh as it seems, it often stems from a genuine desire to preserve "truth" and the orthodoxy of the community. But this mindset also contributes and significantly amplifies cynicism and burn-out. Since all of my teaching and spirituality came from one perspective—one theological bias—and since everyone who surrounded me believed the same things, any inkling of divergence felt as if I was abandoning my community. And in some sense I *was*. I *was* abandoning our singular unified mindset and had become determined to discover and strive to understand the perspectives of those who believed differently from us.

Some people have no interest in looking beyond the position that they have inherited. But I have come to believe that an increasing number of people in my generation likes to have all of the possible views presented to us to enable us to choose which best fits our understanding and experience. For me at least, visiting and having friends in different communities of faith around my school became my saving grace. As I became exposed to perspectives that were significantly different from the community that surrounded me, I found myself compelled toward a deeper faith—partially because the ideas were truly interesting and exciting, and partially because I really just wanted to be *different* from the rest of my community at Moody.

My second life-altering sophomore year experience was a cure for what had become a rather severe "know-it-all" syndrome. As a freshman, I came in with my guns blazing as a Calvinist ready to debate and convince everyone that *my* point of view and *my* nuanced theological perspective was the *most* right. I would take on senior theology majors in theological debate "for fun" and was very vocal in calling out "here-

tics" among us as if it were a sport. Looking back, I believe this heightened sense of pride and arrogance came from my previous over-af-
firmed position within my church community at home. Not that their
affirmation was bad, but over the years it had gone to my head.

Eventually, I ended up in a meeting with the Dean of Students to
discuss my theological compatibility with the college. After this experience, I finally had my bubble popped and my head seriously deflated. I
realized, like so many other students, that I really *didn't* have all the
answers. Reflecting on my debates with the ruthless seniors, I realized
that I didn't know as much as I thought I knew and that I should
perhaps learn to shut up and listen. I became committed to listening,
processing, and offering opinion instead of proclaiming "fact."
Throughout the rest of my career in college, instead of engaging in
debate and arguments, I made sport of watching the incoming freshmen get themselves into theological debates and then get completely
destroyed by upperclassmen and professors. It was reassuring to see
that I was neither alone in my arrogance, nor was I alone in my newfound deflation. It seemed to be a regular, even essential, aspect of the
college experience.

REAL RELATIONSHIPS

Ultimately, the biggest part of the college experience isn't spirituality or
even education; it's relationships. I know that this sounds cliché. But
the relationships that I formed in college helped shape me into the man
that I am today, and I hope that they will be with me for the rest of my
life. These people journeyed with me, struggled with me, got in trouble
with me, and helped me to become a better and more whole person.

On my first night living in my new dorm at Moody during my freshman year, I bumped into a guy who lived a few rooms down from me.
His name was Clark and he was from Canada—a fact that he made
abundantly clear within the first three seconds of introducing ourselves.
As I talked to Clark, I was caught off guard in the best way possible. You
see, Clark didn't at all fit the stereotype of the average Bible college
student. Our friendship was sealed one night a few weeks into the
semester when we decided we were going to attend a student led twen-
ty-four-hour prayer gathering for the city of Chicago. Clark and I met

up and headed downstairs to meet the group for the prayer meeting. Within an hour both of us had snuck off and were sitting in the hallway outside of our dorm rooms where we talked nonstop for the next six hours learning all of the details about each other's lives. When the sun began to rise, we both headed downstairs to get free breakfast with those who had actually stayed up all night to pray. (I know, we're terrible!)

Over the next four years, Clark and I would almost start a church with each other, colead a youth group together, started the radio show together, and spent many nights praying, laughing, and crying with each other. The friendship that we developed helped me get through many incredibly difficult periods of my college life. Friendships like these have helped form me deeply. Classes are important for intellectual growth, but friends are essential for the rest.

Then there is the world of dating. For most young people who end up in Bible College, one of the more primary goals in attending is not actually to study to earn a degree. Far from it. In the evangelical subculture, college is seen as a pivotal period in which young Christian men and women go to find each other to get married. Depending on how this goes for you, this can either be an amazing experience (you find your spouse!) or an incredibly depressing and discouraging season (you don't). I entered Moody certain that within the next four years I would be married. Yet, here I sit four years later, never having gone on a *single date* during my time in college. (It's embarrassing to admit.) Yet, nearly all of the friends who I've made over my time at Moody are either engaged or married today, for better or for worse.

College, for most of us, is a hormonal playground where we are always on the prowl seeking the "right one." This leads many guys and girls to treat romantic relationships either as a game or entirely too seriously. Many guys have an entire Rolodex of girls that they have dated over the four short years of their college career. Still others dated one or two people and were engaged within six months and married within a year. While many in a certain corner of the Christian world see this trend as normal and good, I'm of the view that many students who get married as a sort of "college goal" may face a difficult future together.

On more than one occasion, as anxiety set in as I looked around at all of my friends dating, getting engaged, and getting married, I was tempted to date out of unhealthy motivations. Dating in college can be a relaxed and enjoyable experience, but only if it's taken *less seriously* rather than *more*. My friends who viewed dating carefully, who took their time, and weren't just looking for a spouse ended up happier in the end. And for those of us who never get involved in the dating game, life goes on for us too.

I survived four years without going on a single "real" date—and not because I am a freak or something either! Instead of jumping into dating, I had to personally learn and grow. Sure, it was sometimes hard to watch my friends, one after one, date and get married. But, for me, college became a time for much needed self-discovery and self-improvement to prepare me for healthy relationships.

A FINAL REFLECTION

It was far too easy to view my college experience at Bible College as something altogether different from the average college or university student's journey of self-discovery. But, looking back, the most noteworthy part of my college experience was that I really *did* learn a great deal about myself. Sure, I didn't become the spiritual supersaint I expected to be by graduation. My life struggles didn't disappear as I had hoped. And, yes, many of my preconceived notions about life, ministry, and my faith were completely demolished. Today, I don't pray ten times a day or have the entire New Testament memorized. I didn't even find the girl of my dreams. But what I did experience was good, and true, and helpful for my personal and spiritual development. Looking back, I made incredible friendships, came to understand myself more fully, and journeyed deeper into discovering who God has made me to be. That alone is worth the price of tuition.

QUESTIONS FOR DISCUSSION

1. Robertson's essay addresses several points at which his expectations of college and his actual experience were drastically different. How can colleges market themselves fairly, describing op-

tions available for students without promising more than they can deliver?

2. It's likely the "Moody bubble" is more pronounced than at some schools, but most college students experience some sort of insulated life that privileges on-campus experiences. How does this reality affect faith development for better or for worse?

4

AFTER PRAYERFUL CONSIDERATION

Becoming a Religious Atheist

Kristi Del Vecchio

Dense, chaotic traffic, bright traditional clothing, and hints of spicy food in the air marked my first few hours in Bangalore. Southern India was nothing short of breathtaking. It was the summer of 2011, and I was traveling with an American organization that provides primary medical care to underserved regions across the globe. I had just completed the most challenging semester of my undergraduate career, but academics and extracurricular activities were only part of my struggles; it was also the year I started to identify as an atheist.

The medical mission experience was intended to help gauge my interest in the health professions. I would be immersed in patient-physician interactions, the challenges of cross-cultural communication, and service to a population I assumed needed assistance. Little did I know that this trip would be a crossroads in my faith journey—a pivotal moment in developing my secular worldview.

Because no members of our American mission team spoke Hindi, our work in India was only made possible by a group of local translators. Over two weeks' time, we grew very close with these local Indian men and women; they were, after all, our lifeline to the culture and the people who surrounded us. During our first few days in Bangalore, I worked with a man named James, a young, charismatic Indian social worker. We worked and joked together throughout the first day of clinic, and I loved his sarcastic sense of humor. As James poked fun at

our inability to eat Indian food properly, I quickly responded that the
unorganized, fast paced traffic left us nearly too nauseous to eat at all!

While we organized health clinics in small villages, James and I
continued to learn more about each other. I asked questions about
Indian culture, the role of women in society, and his experience as a
social worker. In turn, James learned more about my life in school, the
weather in Minnesota, and my goals beyond graduation. The longer we
worked together, the more we became comfortable asking questions
about each other's personal lives.

The topic of religion eventually surfaced, and James mentioned cas-
ually that he was a Christian. India is predominantly Hindu, and only
about 2.3 percent of the population identify with the Christian tradition. Because the United States is often portrayed as a Christian country, I think that James expected to further connect through a shared
religious identity. The question finally came: "Kristi, I take it you're
interested in humanitarian work because you're a Christian?"

I felt my stomach drop before stumbling through an answer.

Upon reflection, I think I was shocked by his question because I had
never before been asked it. Most find the Christian call to love one's
neighbor as a "given," demanding little personal explanation from
Christians themselves. That raised the question: why would I feel the
need to do so as a non-Christian? I answered James's question quickly
and cautiously, stumbling around words like *atheist* and concepts like,
". . . but I still like to serve." To be honest, I wasn't really sure, and
James, of course, was just as confused with my answer as I was. After
that afternoon of conversation, James began working more closely with
other team members throughout the duration of our stay.

I was lucky enough to grow up in a Catholic home in Mobile, Ala-
bama, and attend private Catholic school. Surrounded by faithful neighbors, family, friends, and classmates, I had only met a handful of people
who weren't Catholic until I moved to Bismarck, North Dakota at the
age of fifteen. During high school, I attended church weekly and can't
remember missing mass more than a few times a year. I loved church.
More specifically, I loved being part of a community with a shared
vision that took the time to reflect on life beyond the daily grind.

Interestingly enough, I started questioning my valued religious roots
in an introductory religion course at a church-related college. At the

end of my freshman year, I was eager to complete "REL100: Christianity and Religious Diversity," a required milestone for every Concordia College student. Because this course took place at a church-related school, I assumed that it would further solidify and inform my Christian faith. (Still a practicing Catholic at this point, I thought my greatest struggle would be to defend myself in a classroom full of Lutherans!)

Never did I expect an academic course to challenge, and eventually redefine, my worldview to such a large extent. The experience took me by complete surprise. For the first time, I was learning about a diversity of worldviews, but also taking a closer look at Christianity and the Bible. Until this point, I hadn't felt compelled to read this foundational text and explore the major premises of Christianity; Catholicism was the tradition I grew up with and never felt the need to question. The more I explored religion and the Christian tradition more specifically, however, the more uncertain I became about my own religious convictions.

Learning the history of Christianity exposed me to the differences between Jesus as portrayed in the Bible, and Jesus as documented in history. Studying Genesis made me marvel at the diversity of God's creation, yet also revealed the often-disputed role of science in the Bible. I often wondered, "did the theory of evolution conflict with the idea of God creating organisms?" Learning the basic tenets of Islam taught me, in many ways, how little I knew of alternative worldviews. Because of this, the faith I had once so eagerly maintained suddenly felt uninformed and foundationless—something I had failed to notice until this point, likely because my views had never before been critically examined. With a newfound sense of groundlessness, I started exploring my own beliefs.

To make up for what felt like lost time, I gorged myself with books on religion the following summer. As a biology major, I explored questions dealing with rationality and scientific materialism; I wrestled with how biological evolution might be compatible with my religious belief system. Could my Christian worldview withstand what I was learning in my biology classes? As I found out, many authors on this topic seemed to think so.

Texts like *Religion in an Age of Science* by Ian Barbour, *Finding Darwin's God* by Kenneth Miller, and *Belief in God in an Age of Science* by John Polkinghorne explored many of the questions with which I struggled. In these texts, I learned how each writer found solace in a

religious worldview that is also informed by scientific rationale. For the
most part, I appreciated this perspective and often felt reassured by
these authors' ideas. My ultimate goal for reading these books, however
unfortunately, was not granted. I would hurry through each text, expecting an answer for how to believe in God and how to account for
evolution, or why Christianity was even the *right* lens with which to
view the world. Although the books navigated these questions, they fell
short of my desire for an ultimate answer. The authors praised the quest
of science while also believing that faith was an essential component in
their quest for truth. I agreed with the former, yet wasn't able to understand what led Barbour, Miller, and Polkinghorne to ultimately take this
leap of faith.

In hindsight, my desire for an ultimate answer was (only a bit) naïve.
I would eventually recognize that even my secular worldview did not
provide answers to all questions regarding the world, the universe, and
everything. More than a Christian lens could, however, humanism
helped me make sense of my experience. I returned to college in the
fall of my sophomore year with fewer answers, but significantly better
questions. I continued to attend mass half-heartedly my sophomore
year, yet listened closely to sermons, engaged people in conversation,
and explored my own convictions more than ever.

While transitioning to atheism, I hadn't experienced a radical "falling
out" with my religion. For a period of time, I would have considered
myself in an unknowing state of agnosticism. As much as I wanted to
turn to "scientific" rationale to explain my nonreligiousness, I came to
find that my own *personal experience* ultimately led to my transition.
Although the exact moment I started to call myself an atheist isn't
concrete, there was a distinct afternoon when taking this leap of faith
finally felt right.

The season was Lent, a Christian time for prayer, reflection, and
reconciliation. There is a strong emphasis on reflective prayer at all
times in the Catholic tradition, yet the stress to ask for forgiveness is
especially present during the season of Lent. Eager to reflect on my
struggle of faithfulness, and to seek the guidance of a priest, I attended
a Wednesday evening reconciliation service at a Catholic church near
my college.

I could tell that it would be a difficult night when I stumbled into the service a half hour late. Thinking that reconciliation services started at 7:30 p.m., I was stunned when the service was already in full swing! Ready to avoid the embarrassment and just go home, I suddenly noticed a priest in the lobby looking slightly anxious as he adjusted his robe. Sensing my embarrassment, he turned to me and said, "Don't worry, I'm late too. . . . I have a feeling God will forgive both of us, though." After a short laugh, he encouraged me to walk into the service with him—through an entrance that happened to face the front of the altar. During this essential time to seek forgiveness, the whole congregation saw that I was late to the party.

As the service came to a close, a number of visiting priests moved to sit in various corners throughout the church, discussing the sins of each person one at a time. Miraculously, I ended up merging into the line of "Father Late," the kind priest that walked with me into the church all of five minutes ago. "Nice to see you again!" he chuckled before I bowed my now-red face to offer the opening prayer. "Bless me Father, for I have sinned. It has been one year since my last confession. My sins are . . . ."

As a child enrolled in Catholic education, I had been told to be as open as possible to the priest about our sins. I listed a few that I found relevant: failing to uphold loving and patient relationships with my family and friends, allowing my studies to take precedence over church attendance, and . . . well . . . not believing in God anymore? Are you allowed to be THAT explicit with a priest?

Rather than saying, "Father, I don't think I believe in God," I just stopped for a moment to collect my thoughts. I looked back up at him and said, "Father, when did you decide that you wanted to dedicate your life to Catholicism?" Straying significantly from the "say-your-sins" rhythm, I think the priest had picked up on my reservation. His answer, somehow, was the reason I was finally able to let go that day. "I used to ask myself that question as well," he said. "But one day, I just knew that it felt right."

After a blessing and a penitence of three Hail Marys, I returned to my pew knowing that atheism finally felt right.

In no time, Humanism became a path of inspiration, guiding the way I hoped to live my life. I found myself doing volunteer work on campus because I felt called to serve my neighbor, and believed that individual action could make the world a better place. I was enthralled by the idea of earthly salvation, growing in faith that humans have the power to live sustainably and take responsibility for environmental stewardship. I recognized my personal responsibility in working toward those goals, which again inspired me to become a vegetarian and commute by bicycle out of concern for the environment. Although I was raised in a Christian tradition that encourages individuals to improve the world around them, atheism and Secular Humanism inspired me in a way Christianity never had.

Many see adopting atheism a "loss" of faith. I often think this is due to the misconception I once maintained: that secular worldviews don't provide for service, engagement, and care for one's neighbors. As I was starting my humanist journey, I yet again stumbled upon new and unexpected sources of inspiration: friends and colleagues from a vast cross section of worldviews. Just as I was learning to live out my own convictions, I encountered people with religious perspectives and practices radically different from mine, living them out in ways I found inspirational. I would later come to understand these interactions to be part of a movement sweeping college campuses across America: interfaith cooperation.

My interfaith journey started when a Lutheran friend of mine named Elise, a woman now pursuing a career as an Evangelical Lutheran Church in America (ELCA) pastor, asked me to share my story at a public event. One afternoon she asked, "Kristi, would you be interested in representing atheism on my women's interfaith panel?" In all honesty, I wasn't. Telling a large group of people that I was an atheist, in a room likely to be filled with Christians, didn't exactly sound exciting! But thanks to Elise's persistence, I ended up speaking on the panel and shared the story of how I came to my secular worldview with students, community members, and Concordia faculty and staff.

Although those gathered might not have fully agreed with what I had to say, many things happened after the event that I hadn't expected. Various attendees told me that they were surprised to be seeing atheism in a more positive light than they had in the past. Many people said they had never met an atheist before, and that they never envisioned them to be "nice." Others simply told me that their preconceived notions about secularism had been altered. That evening, I learned about the power of breaking stereotypes through sharing my story.

My interfaith journey continued as others challenged *my own* misconceptions about their religious and nonreligious traditions. After the women's interfaith panel, I started to attend meetings and events held by a new organization called the Better Together Interfaith Alliance—a campaign housed under the national interfaith movement piloted by the Interfaith Youth Core (IFYC). In no time, I was sent to an Interfaith Leadership Institute, where professionals from IFYC trained college students to create a movement where religious and nonreligious traditions can serve as a bridge, rather than a barrier.

At the Interfaith Leadership Institute (ILI), I was trained with students from colleges around the United States and met countless people who orient around religion differently. In my cohort alone, I was among Muslims, Buddhists, Jews, atheists, Baha'i practitioners, and multiple denominations of Christianity. My experiences at the ILI, and my following year as a "coach" for IFYC, taught me that though our faith convictions were different, we were united in our desire to work toward the betterment of humanity.

My friend and fellow IFYC coach, Balpreet, wore a turban that extended at least eight inches from the top of her head. The first time I saw her, I watched curiously as she spoke to a stranger in the dinner line about the Sikh tradition. Because she exhibited such openness as to her appearance, I once asked, "Balpreet, why do you choose to wear a turban as a Sikh woman?" Balpreet was happy to answer any and all of my curious questions. She said, "The discipline of the Sikh faith is for all genders. All people wearing turbans do so to visually show their dedication to nonviolence and peace." True to the tradition's history, Balpreet took this commitment seriously in the most challenging of circumstances.

During the year we were coaches, Balpreet's kindness and generosity was tested beyond any expectation. Because Balpreet had facial hair and wore a turban, a Reddit user uploaded a photo of her with the caption, "I'm not sure what to conclude from this." Rather than responding with hurt or anger, Balpreet explained that her religion stresses the beauty of her created body, rather than the alteration of it. She explained in the post's comments:

> Yes, I'm a baptized Sikh woman with facial hair. Yes, I realize that
> my gender is often confused and I look different than most women.
> However, baptized Sikhs believe in the sacredness of this body—it is
> a gift that has been given to us by the Divine Being (which is gender-
> less, actually) and, must keep it intact as a submission to the divine
> will. . . . Sikhs do not reject the body that has been given to us.[1]

Because of her sincere explanation despite such a rude intention, Balpreet was recognized in multiple news reports for her unyielding generosity. I was in awe of Balpreet's actions, but I certainly wasn't the only
one—she was soon named the "Person of the Year" by *Huffington Post
Religion*! During one of our online Google chats after this incident, I
remember telling Balpreet how beautifully she responded to the incident on Reddit. She responded, "I was just doing what I thought to be
right."

Like Balpreet, other religious students in the IFYC coach program
inspired me as a nonreligious person. Masood, a Sunni Muslim man
with contagious laughter, quickly became a friend of mine after we
discovered a shared passion for the musician Sufjan Stevens. During
our coach training at IFYC, Masood consistently demonstrated an important virtue in interfaith conversations: sincere listening and questioning. I watched Masood during an exercise called "hot topics" as he
role-played a conversation about the complexity and diversity of the
Islamic tradition. During the exercise, Masood patiently approached
stereotypes about Islam as a "violent tradition" that "suppresses wom-
en," and sought to dialogue about these misconceptions without conflict.

I once asked Masood how he was able to be patient with people who
have such negative feelings about the Islamic tradition. Rather than
blaming Americans for their ignorance, Masood chose to respond with
empathy: "It's often the case that Americans only know Muslims
through the 9/11 attack . . . and if that were my experience, I might be
hesitant toward the tradition as well." As a secular person who faces
media-based stereotypes about "amorality" and "ungodliness," I knew I
could learn from Masood's calm and level-headed patience toward
those who viewed him with suspicion. I quickly learned from Masood

---

1. Lindy West, "Reddit Users Attempt to Shame Sikh Woman, Get Righteously
Schooled," September 26, 2012, accessed July 24, 2014, http://jezebel.com/5946643/reddit-
users-attempt-to-shame-sikh-woman-get-righteously-schooled .

that generous listening and sharing in interfaith conversations go a long way.

After training as an IFYC coach that summer, I started my senior year of college as a copresident for Concordia's Better Together Interfaith Alliance. My partner for the year would be Sarah, an active ELCA Lutheran and dedicated interfaith leader. Throughout our year of teamwork and leadership in the group, Sarah's support for all of the religious and nonreligious students on Concordia's campus amazed me. Sarah believed that two unrecognized student organizations, an Evangelical Christian group and the Secular Student Community, should be supported by our ELCA campus administrators. Although I was thankful for Sarah's support, I never quite realized the extent of it.

One afternoon at a Better Together meeting, Sarah described a situation from earlier that week, when she had been giving a campus tour to prospective students. When passing by the chapel, Sarah highlighted the worship opportunities and Christian affiliated organizations on campus. One prospective student, however, asked what opportunities were available for students who weren't members of the ELCA. Stressing the campus's newfound efforts toward interfaith cooperation, Sarah stated, "Concordia is working to recognize both Evangelical Christians and secular students on campus, and we are moving in this direction *because* we are an ELCA affiliated school." Sarah didn't believe that Concordia would truly be a campus of interfaith cooperation until everyone's voice—ELCA or not ELCA—could be heard. In Sarah, I saw unfailing dedication to community and hospitality.

Interfaith cooperation created a space where, for the first time, I was *supposed* to build mutually inspiring relationships with people of different religious and nonreligious backgrounds. I found myself turning to these examples to best embody my own values: Balpreet for kindness, Masood for patience, and Sarah for radical hospitality. These and other individuals challenged me to grow more into my "faith tradition," and redefined whom I saw as a neighbor. From these experiences, I saw interfaith work as a vehicle for practicing humanitarian efforts with others. I realized that the differences between our worldviews didn't have to be the end of the story. In fact, I wondered, would I not be a *better* atheist, a better humanist, if I chose to work with people from other worldviews to make the world a better place? I continued doing interfaith work because I was an atheist and humanist—not despite being so.

The medical mission to southern India taught me more than I ever expected. Meeting James would prepare me for countless other people I would come to know, as I continued to pursue conversations about faith for the rest of my time in college. From the conversation James and I had, and the unfortunate separation it brought in our friendship, I learned how to discuss my convictions in a way that resonates with others. Although my journey abroad was only a few years ago, I feel more compelled than ever to engage with people from different backgrounds.

My faith journey is not all that different from many others. Even today, I experience growth, questioning, challenges, and even doubt. Encountering thought-provoking ideas within philosophy, religion, and science continue to evolve my worldview, as well as the way I try to live out my convictions. A secular worldview *does* make the most sense to me, but it *doesn't* answer all of my questions about the world, the universe, and everything in them. But for me, theistic worldviews don't answer them either. Personal experiences with life's surprises and uncertainties, even as an atheist, have taught me to be more comfortable with the ambiguity of my own human experience.

Although aspects of my humanist practice may change over time, I have found it to be the foundation that best sustains me. With new experiences and challenges in my postgraduate life, I certainly hope that my worldview *does* continue to evolve. Like the many religious people around me, I am eager to continue developing my nonreligious worldview in a way that will help me best serve humanity— hopefully alongside the Sikh, Muslim, Christian, and countless other neighbors who continue to inspire me.

QUESTIONS FOR DISCUSSION:

1. While Del Vecchio researched rational, scholarly arguments for both atheism and religious faith, she writes that ultimately she claimed her identity as an atheist and humanist because of per-

sonal experience. What connections do personal experience and scientific rationale have to your worldview?

2. The essay mentions the stereotypes many people have of atheists. Does Del Vecchio's story dispel any for you? At what times, and how, have you seen religious stereotypes dismantled?

3. Del Vecchio reflects on what she has learned from friends and mentors. She's relied on, "Balpreet for kindness, Masood for patience, and Sarah for radical hospitality." From whom have you learned (holy) wisdom?

Section II

Who Am I? Who Is God? What Am I to Do? Stories of Call

A student stopped me in the hall recently and asked if she could set up an appointment to talk soon. "Sure," I said, "Anything particular on your mind?"

"Not really. . . . I just need to figure out my life."

As a professor, it's a common privilege to meet with students about enormously important decisions concerning classes, majors, job prospects, graduate school, and relationships. Each of these topics raises students' anxiety levels. Students feel pressure to, indeed, figure out their entire lives by the time they turn twenty-two. They commonly misjudge minor setbacks as more devastating than they truly are. And, for many students, questions of vocation and life's purpose are mixed-up in a confusing combination of "God's will," their parents' expectations, and their own self-understanding. Section II considers such college challenges.

Lydia Hawkins's essay, "Studying, Praying, Seeking: A Spiritual Tapestry" reveals uncommon reflection on these matters and wisely notes the interrelation of faith and learning. In "Why in God's Name Am I Here?" Rick Reiten shares his college faith transition featuring an important variety of voices—and a night under the stars. In North Carolina, Hillary Martinez struggled with similar questions and found clarity one summer, while Anna DeWeese, in Arkansas, learned to shake the "pastor's kid" label at a college of the church. Surely none of these students' discernment was complete at graduation, but their stories of faithful questioning should help others continue the process of seeking to respond to God's call.

5

STUDYING, PRAYING, SEEKING

A Spiritual Tapestry

Lydia Hawkins

Reflecting upon my time as a college student, it is impossible to divorce faith and spirituality from the rest of my collegiate experience. The different threads were woven together so tightly it's difficult to discern where one begins and the other ends. Together, these strands made my college experience a spiritual tapestry, alive with texture and interweaving colors. My faith affected my thinking about academic and occupational pursuits, while these pursuits affected my faith. My collegiate activities influenced how I prayed, and my prayer life influenced my collegiate activities. As I learned about myself, others, and the world during my college experience, I grew in my relationship with God. Guided by a sense of vocation as a student, a spirituality that involves the mind, and a journey toward discovering and becoming my truest self, I experienced a faith pilgrimage integrated with my college career.

A SCHOLASTIC CALLING

The employee in the registrar's office took my withdraw request form, checking to ensure all the appropriate information was there. She handed it back to me, noting that I had not filled out the "Reasons for Withdraw." I thought a moment before filling in my response and handed it back. She looked back up at me in surprise as she read "not challenging enough" scrawled out on the form.

I approached my freshman year of college with an initial sense of seriousness for my studies. I considered that I only had four short years to experience something for which many never get the chance. I understood how blessed I was to attend the liberal arts university of my choice only through financial assistance. Plus, I have a natural inclination toward pursuit of knowledge. These combined motivations helped me to employ what we discussed in one of my freshman English classes: the attitude not to just *receive* an education, but to *claim* it. It was not mere gratitude or academic interest providing this continued conviction throughout my university years, however; it was the link between my student life and my Christian life. Being a student was my calling. Viewing my educational experience in this light affected everything from my prayer life, to what I studied, to how I spent my time.

Discussions in Church Vocations Symposium first shone light on this sense of vocation. There a small group of students met weekly for a meal, theological discourse, and prayer. Many of the students who attended were considering living out their future vocations as pastors, counselors, church musicians, nurses, or social workers. Paradoxically, it was in this group of students who were taking seriously the task of preparing for their future vocations that we were reminded not to neglect our present one.

One of these conversations stemmed from an article that influenced the rest of my college career: "Go with God: An Open Letter to Young Christians on Their Way to College," by Stanley Hauerwas. This article moved my motivation beyond just myself and career goals toward the larger implication that the Church needs its students to do well in school. Hauerwas helped me to interweave my studies and my faith; he asserted that no matter what we ended up doing with our lives, now was the time for Christian students to develop the intellectual skills needed by the Church to build up the Body of Christ. While many students I met in college begrudgingly attended as a means to an end, Hauerwas's article and other Church Vocations discussions helped me focus on my current experience instead of the goal of building a résumé, a degree, and a career.

The integrated motivation to claim my education for knowledge's sake and as a Christian duty imposed an amount of seriousness to all the decisions I would make. Knowing my transitory opportunity was precious and part of my vocation, I preserved what one of my professors noted as "stewardship of the mind." I approached the time of class registration with prayer for wisdom in course selection. I sought out former students' advice in professor choices, examined professors' book selections, and contacted prospective class professors with questions. My resolute approach determined my course track in college.

This conviction came forward most strongly as I struggled my freshman and sophomore years with the decision for a major. Having a heart for eventually working with people in interpersonal settings and having the conviction to grow as a thinker, I oscillated between options. If I chose the social work or ministry majors, I would receive a practice-based education to prepare me for a future career but would not have the schedule space for more academic classes. If I chose theology or psychology, I would deal with conceptual ideas related to my future field and grow as a thinker but not gain the practical knowledge in the classroom. After much prayer, anxiety, and phone calls from my parents asking, "What is your major this week?" I reached a conclusion. I could not justify spending my calling as a student in classes where I felt I was just being trained for a career instead of also training to be a better thinker. After these two years of indecision, I settled upon the pursuit of theological and psychological studies. This choice allowed me the freedom to truly grow as a thinker through my primary studies and through the space available for elective philosophy, English, and art classes as well.

Considering my education a vocation did not allow me to compartmentalize my faith and my studies, nor did it push me to the other extreme of only seeking classes that had a Christian approach. It rather meant that everything about my student experience had to be viewed in the light of Christ. As I walked past the beautiful Chapel of the Resurrection in the center of campus on the way to class, the chapel served as a bold reminder of my daily attempt to discern Truth, whether I was in a biology, sociology, or theology class. It served as motivation for my daily fight to sharpen my skills for the sake of the Church and Gospel, whether they involved the abilities to speak Spanish, counsel clients, or just to think critically. My whole school week was about living out my Christian faith as I exited morning chapel, attended classes, rose from prayer, pored over challenging texts, or engaged in stimulating discussion with peers.

FAITH SEEKING UNDERSTANDING

My freshman English course began with an "Origins" section where we reflected on our own "origin stories" alongside the origin stories of different populations. As we explored the origin myths of different cultures, I was perturbed to see the Genesis creation story studied alongside these texts. I was unsettled as something I had accepted as undeniably sacred and true was introduced as allegorical literature by my atheist professor. When encountering this text I thought I had known so well from my faith tradition, I was further dismayed to realize there were two different creation stories in Genesis and the juicy, red apple I had thought was there was nowhere to be found! Introduction to this class section led to the need to explore my *faith origins* as I began to realize much of my faith was based on beliefs I had accepted without examination and could not explain.

I realized that my Christianity was a product of my context as I encountered a Muslim floormate who viewed Jesus as a prophet and my Muslim friend from Saudi Arabia who was more charitable and devout than most Christians I knew. My inability to explain my faith surfaced in conversations with people of differing opinions: from the agnostic who outwitted me in philosophy class to the new interactions with Christians of other denominations. The need to examine beliefs that had not been relevant before rose to the surface as I walked alongside multiple friends struggling through their sexual orientations, their places within the church, and the supposedly loving reactions of Christians. Multiple classes gave me new perspectives on scripture, which I had so unknowingly allowed to shape my faith, unexplored.

While I found communities and resources to feed me spiritually in the Catholic Church near campus, my lingering high school struggles with Catholicism only deepened. As my unease with the tradition continued, I explored other denominations just to arrive at the same level of dissatisfaction. My concerns quickly spread from Catholicism to the value of church in general. At times, I doubted not only the faith community but faith at all. Realizing the lack of Jesus in my faith foundations, I wondered if I would be better off a Jew than a Christian. As I continually encountered ideas, faiths, lifestyles, and knowledge that contradicted the faith I had held, I acknowledged the pressing need to step back from my faith in order to examine it. In a painful but rewarding process I had to deconstruct my faith and ideologies in order to start rebuilding anew.

I entered a process of discarding and preserving beliefs with a sense of urgency as I knew my faith was on the line. I take note of how very central the mind was to this stage in my journey. The catalyst of my shaken faith was not due to the absence of God's presence and mercies or due to traumatic events that made me question God's goodness. Rather, my struggles were initiated by unanswered questions that left me unsure of why I believed or lived the way I did. I eventually found comfort in reasoning through the voids. In the midst of this searching I found myself supported by professors, pastors, and campus ministers. Even though I was full of doubt, I found safe-havens in theology classes, places I felt my faith was at least momentarily safe. I slowly began to reconstruct my faith, replacing old concepts with new ones. Just as my faith had been deconstructed by the mind, my faith was also reconstructed through the mind.

As I began reassembling my faith through reason, however, I ran into the danger of allowing my reason to completely determine my faith. While I grew stronger in faith and closer to God through contemplation, I also found myself hiding my faith behind knowledge. I noticed myself beginning to spend more time thinking *about* God than allowing myself to *experience* God. I began to feel prideful about my type of faith: I looked down on faiths that seemed emotion-based, fluctuating with the moods and circumstances of current situations instead of grounded in stable beliefs. Attempting not to be associated with "those type of people," I used knowledge of God, Scripture, and doctrine to define my faith. I only cautiously and occasionally revealed what "felt" like movements of God in my life, answers to prayers, or experiences in God's presence.

Once again influenced by the classroom, I was able to integrate this faith divide between my heart and my mind. Invited by two of my admired theology professors to use my own experience in papers, I began to feel more comfortable viewing the experiential as a valid source of faith knowledge. This notion was further supported in a class on Christian spirituality as we ventured through primary sources of influential spiritual leaders in the Christian tradition. Through the thought-provoking discussions and encounters with these holy role models, I found it impossible not to incorporate my own experience into the class. Encounters with Thomas Merton, C. S. Lewis, Augustine, Teresa of Avila, Thomas Aquinas, and countless professors and friends throughout my college years guided me to embrace this important notion: I could be both intellectual and spiritual. Through reason's role in the deconstruction, reconstruction, and integration of my faith, I have learned faith and reason are deeply complementary. Yet, reason does not separate itself from, or even lessen, the spiritual aspects of faith. I have come to understand that the mind, for me, is a pathway toward closer relationship with God and discerning God's movements in my life.

THE INWARD JOURNEY

Part of my experience as a college student was the introduction to the new freedom and burden of *choice*. Suddenly, I was confronted with many opportunities able to influence me and my future. With newfound independence and a myriad of directions, the decision-making process became weightier than my high school experience where course lists and decisions were ultimately monitored by higher authorities. As I wrestled with new questions about what I should major in, who I should date, or where I should be employed or study abroad, I realized the need to wrestle with how to discern the answers to these questions.

Beginning my freshman year of college declared a Youth Ministry major, I was looking forward to the campus minister at my new church becoming a mentor. Shortly after I met him, I asked why he ended up where he did. Expecting a heart-warming story of how he found his "calling," I was surprised when he simply stated that he was interested in the career and thought he would be good at it. I walked away from the conversation deeply disappointed. This minister could not be a role model to me; he hadn't even been called by God to his position.

My reaction to this conversation was a reflection of how I viewed discernment and calling. At the time, I understood the discernment process as the attempt to know how to follow "God's will" in big decisions. Operating under the idea that "God's will" for me was a strictly laid out plan, the decision-making process was exhausting. Burdened by self-inflicted anxiety, I felt hopeless about the requirement to choose "correctly" and guilty about whether I actually had. My college experience necessitated and guided me toward a healthier understanding of God's will and the practice of discerning it.

Sitting in a pew at Wednesday evening services, a confused freshman looking for answers and hope, I received the gift of two memorable sermons. The first sermon debunked the idea that God wants us to find "the One" and marry them, rather proposing that there are many compatible people on this earth with whom we could choose to work at the covenant of marriage. While many unmoved students sat around me, nodding in agreement at the startling words of the pastor, I felt first a wave of shock—*there isn't "the One?!"*—and then relief at something I had been waiting for someone to tell me was OK to believe.

A few weeks later, another sermon used the Garden of Eden as an allegory for the liberty we could employ in our own decision-making processes in college. The pastor spoke about how God ordered the man and woman not to eat from the forbidden tree, but otherwise, permitted them to be "free to eat from any of the trees in the garden." More relief followed as I thought about the burden lifted from not only dating decisions, but *all* decisions. These sermons served as catalysts for exploration of what "God's will" for me really meant at a time when the abundant choices of the collegiate experience made the topic imminent.

Continuing conversations throughout my collegiate years with friends, ministers, spiritual directors, and in prayer opened my eyes to a broader view of God's will for my life. I began to truly embrace the freedom that comes with employing free will. The guilt was removed in my decision-making processes as my definition of this "plan" expanded from a narrow, guilt-ridden path to a broad, liberating garden in which there hang many delightful fruits. My image of God broadened from a demanding God who is micro-managing every step of the way, to a loving God who gives me many choices that still fall within His will.

I have come to believe that ultimately God's will for me is to become the best version of myself, living out my unique personhood in the holiest ways possible. While I now understand this is God's will for everyone, I also recognize that the calling to be the best version of ourselves looks different for each person. A new understanding of what it means to follow God's will and call led to a reassessment of my understanding of what it means to pray about these concepts, to practice discernment.

As my understanding of God's will broadened, so did my approach to discernment practices: I began seeking wisdom and guidance for direction, as opposed to a specific answer, decision by decision. Before, I had anxiously sought (and rarely found) the yes or no answer from God as to whether a certain decision was part of His outlined "plan" for me. Now, I attempt to examine my motives and to weigh the rationality of different decisions through the use of reason. I practice discernment by listening to the encouragement and wisdom of other members of the body of Christ (whether living persons or encountered in written works), and by examining what would be the greatest good for both others and me. I remain attentive to which doors open, which seem not to budge, and which reveal lasting peace.

Although I no longer searched for specific decisions God expected me to make, the remaining possibilities for my "calling" remained daunting. I was no longer stressing out about whether summer job Choice A or Choice B would lead me to the Choice D I was supposed to make two years down the road. Nevertheless, I still asked big questions about how best to use my gifts for the glory of God and the good of His creations. Am I best fit for marriage or the single life? Should I go on to an academically rigorous field in graduate school? Should I pursue something right after graduation in the field of social services? With my looming future after college seeming so abstract, I assumed I was going to need *big* help from God, aside from just wisdom in discernment, to know how to move forward.

While I was waiting for some lightning, a vision, or even just a gentle whisper in regard to my calling, I was instead struck by a liberating idea. I realized that perhaps I would not be directed by grandiose guidance from beyond, but could, instead, look within. I began to understand that God can guide us through our desires. This notion first formed from my introduction to *The Spiritual Exercises*, by Saint Ignatius of Loyola, through a theology class. This guided mediation is intended to aid someone in discerning a decision or vocation through the use of their desires and reason. In continuing conversations with the theology professor who taught the class and a psychology professor trained in Ignatian exercises, I found comfort in this new way to think about God's calls. When thinking about discerning callings, I resonated with the way James Martin, a Jesuit priest, explains it in *My Life with the Saints*:

> That's what "the call" was for me. Today many people, even believers, think that a call to the priesthood or religious life is something of an otherworldly experience—hearing voices, seeing visions. But for me it was merely a simple attraction, a heartfelt desire, a sort of emotional pull—a happy inability to think of anything else. [1]

I stopped hoping to receive a voice from God, like Mother Teresa, that would tell me what to do with my life. I stopped worrying whether I had seen all the "signs" in my life that had been pointing me in the right direction. My new understanding of God's calling for my life was about becoming the best version of myself, guided by the interests and desires I was given. The conversation with the campus minister who had followed his interests and gifts into a career was no longer seen as disappointing, but indeed a story about his calling. And with this new understanding of calling, the ability to better understand myself became a necessary part of the discernment process. My focus in discernment shifted from, "What is God's big plan for my life?" to, "Who am I called to be?"

AN INTEGRATED WHOLE

Aware of this spiritual exploration, it's impossible to divorce my college years from my faith. For me, the collegiate experience was so conducive to such exploration. As my college years provided an environment with ample opportunities to explore, they allowed me to grow to better understand myself in a new light. In college, I discovered within myself a growing heart for service, social justice, and people. Through affirmations from new relationships, I had fresh insight into what others saw as my gifts and possible ways to live those out. From the freedom I had available to create what my four years of college would look like, I

---

1. James, Martin, *My Life with the Saints* (Chicago: Loyola Press, 2006), 59.

began to see more clearly my true interests and desires in the way those years took shape.

Not long from now, I will not remember what I learned in certain classes in college. But long from now, I will remember what I learned about myself, about how to relate to others, and about how to think about what I believe. This type of self-knowledge continually draws me closer toward being who I am—the person God has called me to be. Furthermore, this type of inward journey continually draws me closer to God. This being said, I cannot separate any of the opportunities that college provided me from my faith; they helped to shape me into who I am, which is so essential to the journey of my spiritual life. And just as I cannot separate college from my faith, I cannot separate faith from my college. It determined what I thought about when I rose, with whom I spent my time and shared my heart, and the classes and even the major I chose. Fundamentally, it was the motivation behind my studies. College, for me, was a spiritual search for an identity—a search that is just the beginning of a lifelong pursuit.

QUESTIONS FOR DISCUSSION

1. Hawkins writes that in college, "being a student was my calling." How might this perspective affect how students see their college studies and extracurricular activities?
2. The process of stepping back and reexamining one's faith is a theme of the essay. When have you undertaken such a process? How did it succeed or falter?
3. Hawkins notes that two sermons, in particular, stood out in her college experience. What sermons, lectures, or presentations from your past have made the most impact on your life?

6

WHY IN GOD'S NAME AM I HERE?

Rick Reiten

Old, small, white, rural country church in northwest Wisconsin. Norwegian Lutheran heritage. Blue-haired ladies. Few children. Pointless confirmation instruction. No youth program. Boring liturgy. Plodding music. Why in God's name am I here?

I grew up in this congregation, attended worship most Sundays, was confirmed in the tenth grade, and never questioned that my faith experience could be any better. But during those last couple of years in high school, as I started figuring out more about myself, started exploring faith questions and practices, I began to suspect there had to be something more inspiring than what this church had offered me. I still wanted "church," but not the church I had growing up. No longer could I handle the unenthusiastic drone of senior citizens who had recited the same prayers, music, and responses for ninety years.

I asked a lot of questions preparing for my exodus out of the Lutheran church, but the questions were only for my own ears. I figured that nobody would have the answers I needed, so why bother telling anyone? The list was extensive. Why is church just for old people? Where do these monotonous words we say every week come from? Why don't we have any excitement or joy? Why does every church event revolve around food? Does anyone actually listen to the sermon? Why does the Bible always contradict itself? Is my church making a difference in the world? In the lives of anyone? I had no answers. I was happy to get away.

I started at the University of Wisconsin–La Crosse in the fall of 2001. Two weeks into college, I wanted to leave. I had trouble connecting with anyone. I thought making friends would be easy since I had a lot in high school. I was easygoing, after all, and had a variety of interests. But after high school, I felt like an outsider searching, desperately, for somewhere to belong. While my roommate hung out with his friends from high school at the university, I could not do the same and felt even more alone. I had been admitted into the athletic training program, seemingly prime territory for friends, but couldn't connect with anyone. I tried the drinking scene, but felt out of place. I thought I had figured out who I was while still in high school, but that identity was being slowly dismantled. I wasn't a quitter, but I didn't think there was any option. Maybe college wasn't for me. I was days away from dropping out and going home.

Then I met Beau. He lived a few doors down—fourth floor Coate Hall—and asked if I wanted to join a Bible study group. I knew I wanted to explore faith a bit, but I figured I'd get to it later. Where was the rush? I was hesitant, skeptical of Beau's invitation. Would it be like my home church? Would I be accepted? But, wanting to succeed at college, needing a lifeline and some friends, I agreed. Beau was a senior, who had been placed by Campus Crusade for Christ (now Cru) in the dorms to minister to freshmen. (Reflecting back on the philosophy of that placement, I feel a bit violated. Was I just a project? Cru theology emphasized "winning" souls for Christ. How authentic was this encounter? Still, I believe his heart was in the right place and I thank God for that relationship.)

To my surprise, I enjoyed Bible study. I quickly realized that I never knew much at all about this book of faith. I was grateful that Beau spent time with me, cared about me, introduced me to others who accepted me. We went to Thursday night worship at Crusade, and it was exciting to worship with three hundred college students. We went to Sunday church services at a community nondenominational church, followed by brunch together back at the campus cafeteria. Beau became a mentor and friend. He taught me how to pray and helped me explore faith and question religion.

As I continued through my freshman year, I experienced many highs and lows of life, but this developing faith was always at the center. Beau, too, was always there, available to listen and guide, to help me through the moments of wrestling. Beau was the first person who helped me connect the abstract, impersonal faith of my high school church experience to concrete everyday life events.

A few months into college, I went home for a visit and caught my longtime girlfriend cheating on me. I knew we had to break up, but I thought the right thing was to forgive and make it work. However, it was an extremely unhealthy relationship that was hurting both of us, and it needed to end. Beau promised me that God loved me enough, and I didn't need a girlfriend to feel valued. He was right.

As much as I was learning about life and faith, I still didn't think I was adequate. One day I was walking on campus and approached by two Mormon missionaries. I had no idea who a Mormon was, or what they believed, but I tried to be confident. I told them I was Christian and proudly read the Bible (I didn't say how new I was at it). They prodded me with questions, and I ended up declaring that John the Baptist wrote the Gospel of John. They laughed at me, and invited me to learn the truth. I was humiliated and ashamed, but Beau continued to change my perspective and encouraged me.

I needed encouragement during that first year, as I struggled with the athletic training program. I enjoyed sports medicine, but didn't feel ready to devote my life to it. Toward the end of the year, I learned that the athletic training program would be cutting ten students from the program, and I wasn't sure what I wanted to do. I didn't want to voluntarily quit, but as always, Beau was there. He suggested that I let the year play out, and see what would be decided, "trusting in God's will" as he put it. I ended up being cut from the program, which meant I had to figure out a new direction and major, but at the same time I felt freer.

When I returned home for spring break my pastor invited me to lead the high school youth on a weekend retreat at the nearby Bible camp. After my Campus Crusade Bible studies, I felt reasonably assured I could handle it, so I agreed. I had come home that week looking for a summer job, and as I left with the youth for camp, I had no leads. I felt deflated. During that weekend God helped me to see another side of living out our faith. It was still hard for me to utter the word "Lutheran" without a little distaste in my mouth, but the Bible camp turned out to be a Lutheran camp that had exciting music, energy, dynamic speaking, and fun people. I connected instantly. At the end of the weekend, the camp director said she needed summer counselors, and knew I would fit in well.

But I wasn't convinced that I could be a camp counselor. Even though the director encouraged me, I found excuses. I questioned if this was the right place, even wondering if I would make enough money to help with college tuition. How would I teach kids about God when I was still really figuring it all out? I wasn't ready to lead a Bible study or worship or devotions. I was acutely aware that only six months prior I thought John the Baptist wrote a gospel! But the most perplexing question was this: how could I teach Lutheran doctrine or confirmation when I wasn't even sure *I* liked it?

I filled out the application, but sat on it for a few weeks. When I was cut from the athletic training program, I realized I didn't have to return in August for fall sports. Then, I got another job offer at a convenience store. I could work at the gas station on the weekends, and make roughly the same amount of money as at camp. If I did both, I could double my summer earnings. I had no more excuses.

That summer of 2002, at Luther Park Bible Camp in Chetek, Wisconsin, was a blur. I was working 127 hours a week at camp (but I got to sleep for some of it) and 16 hours at the convenience store. As we went through staff training—a two week period before campers arrived—I had some major moments of doubt. I enjoyed the company of my peers and colleagues, but I still wasn't so sure about the Lutheran part. I held tightly to my influence from Beau and Campus Crusade—the intimate small groups and prayer circles, faith testimonies and engaging worship. But by the end of staff training, even as I was anxious about campers arriving, I began to trust this new group of friends. Even as I questioned participating in the Lutheran tradition, these people, these new friends embodied a faith I came to admire. It became a glorious summer of discovery. I grew to appreciate the following:

- The hymns, liturgy, ancient creeds, and prayers come from a deep rooted practice in the church, and a lot straight from scripture itself.
- The Lutheran church doesn't claim to have all the answers but is one expression of faith. Nobody ever pressured me to come back to my Lutheran roots.
- The sacraments had real power.

- A community of faith, working together in love, is a beautiful thing.

Ultimately I realized that, as I worked with campers, my own understanding of faith was strengthened at the same time. While this felt a bit of a paradox, it was my experience. While my confidence in the faith grew, I was quite surprised when some close friends prompted me to explore seminary. Seminary!

To say that that summer I resisted the notion of seminary is to put things mildly. If I was worried about camp pay for a summer, how could I do ministry full-time as a career and *ever* support myself (or a family)? My priorities included 1) enjoying college, 2) graduating, and 3) finding a suitable job that paid well. Who would want to change such a tried-and-true plan? Not me. Yet, the prodding from those friends never ended. In a place where I initially felt uncomfortable, I found people who supported and encouraged me. I trusted their urging, wrestling with what seminary might mean for me.

One night, as campers were sleeping, I snuck out to a field, lay down, and stared at the sky. It was time to have an honest conversation with God. Part of me felt called to be a pastor, but I questioned my qualifications and adequacy. Why in God's name am I thinking about seminary? God didn't answer with a loud voice or blinding light, but my anxiety calmed, and my discernment continued. I would need prayerful support and many faith-filled reminders along the way, but by the end of the summer my life plans had changed.

In less than a year I went from "Lutherans stink, get me outta here," to "nondenominational free" and back to "Lutherans are kind of cool." I journeyed from "hesitant Bible study attendee" to "Bible study leader," from "athletic trainer dream" to "(gasp) one-day pastor," from "I want to leave college" to "I can't wait to get back to UWL and share my good news with friends!"

As I soaked up the joy and excitement of the summer, along the way I realized that I had more fun in the bone-tiring 127 hours of ministry with kids than I did in the drudgery of the gas station—no matter what the paycheck every other Friday told me. I found a new hobby in the delight of playing guitar, and camp offered me an environment to learn quickly. And it turns out that one of those friends who supported me in this new call (often reminding me that God first calls us, and *then* qualifies) was a lot of fun to be with . . . plus she was pretty cute. Today, she is my best friend and wife of eight years.

When I went back to La Crosse, though I was becoming comfortable with this call to ministry and a return to the Lutheran roots, my friends were still part of Campus Crusade. I didn't want my Lutheran faith to negatively affect those relationships. Soon, however, reality struck. And it hurt.

My college friends greeted my camp stories with blank stares and heartbreaking comments.

"What happened to you?"

"The Lutheran church practices the wrong kind of baptism."

"You are dating a girl from Luther College? That just isn't right."

"Crusade is about truly following Jesus—not just a source of friends."

Even Beau, my friend, encourager, mentor—challenged me to further explore Lutherans and their "faithless" practices like infant baptism. I was so excited to share my summer, but these comments drove me to tears and back to my dorm room shared with two other Crusade "friends."

A year prior I sat alone with faith questions filling my soul, searching for true friends. Now, I was back to the same place. But I realized it wasn't exactly similar, that God truly had moved me forward and had given me the opportunity I wanted—to wrestle with faith and come to a clearer understanding of myself and my call. I also realized I wasn't alone. I had a community of friends from camp who understood me more than I imagined was possible. They supported me and encouraged me. So, with the confidence that came from God knows where, I walked away from Campus Crusade and the relationships that had saved me from dropping out of college.

My eyes scan the webpage of listings. Intervarsity. Catholic Newman Center. Crossroads. *Lutheran Campus Ministry*. Really? Hmm, maybe it is worth a shot. I'll wander over there after class.

Wow, the house doesn't look like much. It's small, run-down, grayish—ugly, really. Maybe I shouldn't even go in. I don't think anyone is there. OK, I'll just knock once.

The young woman who answers the door greets me with a warm smile. She explains she's a resident, so this is the right place, the Lutheran Campus Ministry house.

There is free dinner and Bible study on Thursday nights. But, eight people show up? What an insignificant number compared to the 350 people worshipping in Graff Main Hall Auditorium with Campus Crusade. Eight people (on a good night!) making homemade dinner, holding a Bible study inside a nondescript house, on a damp, drafty, living room floor. Maybe I will fit in.

And I did.

I am pastor in an old, small, white, rural country church in southern Wisconsin. Same Norwegian Lutheran heritage. The blue-haired ladies are young at heart. We have a few more children. Pointless confirmation instruction? Hopefully not. Youth program? Yep! Boring liturgy and plodding music—no more. I give thanks, for in God's name, I am here.

QUESTIONS FOR DISCUSSION:

1. Reiten met Beau at just the right moment and Beau served as a friend and mentor throughout Reiten's freshman year. Who has served as a mentor in your life?
2. Have you had experiences with campus ministry—Cru, denominational ministries, other? What do your experiences have in common? What about them is distinct?
3. How has your faith changed over your lifetime? What experiences have brought about these changes?

7

LIVING IN THE CENTER OF GOD'S WILL

Hillary Martinez

I arrived at Duke University sure that in the first few months of my freshman year God would reveal his plan for my life, leading me to choose the appropriate major and career path in a timely, efficient manner. All of the adults I knew well seemed to have a strong sense of who they were and how they should best use their gifts. So, I expected that one day soon, a few wise words and moments of silent reflection would somehow reveal in beautiful simplicity who I was and what I was supposed to do with my life. As my freshman year progressed, I was surprised and confused when no such clear "revelation" arrived.

Since God was apparently remaining silent, I decided to take the matter of discovering my vocation in my own hands. My plan was simple: If I could understand the nuances of my character to a T, I'd surely be able to pinpoint what work God had in store for me. So I took personality tests, made appointments with career counselors, and constantly questioned my friends and family about the merits of various career paths. Throughout this process, I gained some insight into my strengths, weaknesses, and gifts, but I was far from reassured. As sophomore year approached, I knew I would soon need to declare a major and participate in the appropriate extracurricular activities and internships for my chosen career path. I found myself envious of friends who declared confidently that they would someday be doctors or engineers or graphic designers. When classmates or friends asked me what I hoped to do, I often just laughed nervously and offered up whatever career came to mind that day. "College administration," I answered, "or maybe nonprofit work?" The test results, personality profiles, and vague advice from friends and acquaintances left me filled with uncertainty and teetering on the edge of anxiety. Nothing seemed clear cut. Would God's plan for my life ever become clear to me? If not, what would happen if I chose the wrong course for my life? Would God rescind blessings from my life and leave me alone, uncertain, and uninspired?

In a bid for clarity, I decided to apply to Duke Chapel's undergraduate summer internship program that focused on calling and vocation. According to the program director, Rev. Keith Daniel, the purpose of the summer internship was to provide time and space for students to enter into a process of discernment around their personal vocation and calling. I couldn't imagine a better time for God, finally, to reveal a perfect plan for my life.

Filled with expectation, I began my internship at a tutoring center in Durham, hoping that God would confirm my current vocational leanings toward education. However, my internship was not the affirming experience that I had expected. Instead of confirming a distinct path for my future, those weeks offered only exhaustion and confusion. I realized I had no idea how to control a classroom of rambunctious sixth-graders. I had trouble understanding the challenges faced by the students who lived in the underserved community around the tutoring center. I struggled to see how my classes at Duke had prepared me to show God's love in a raw, real world.

My supervisor Natalie fascinated me: she had given up the prospect of a secure career as an elementary school teacher to run the after-school tutoring program at the Life Center, working other jobs on the side to make ends meet. Most of my peers at Duke were on the fast track to secure and lucrative jobs; I couldn't imagine my classmates—or myself for that matter—making the sacrificial career decisions that Natalie had chosen. When I asked Natalie more about her career choices, she explained to me that she believed her work was ministerial, a conception that challenged my traditional notions of the parameters of "ministry."

Until that summer, I assumed that only a few people were actually called to ministry: missionaries, pastors, and perhaps some famous Christian thinkers. But, one afternoon, as Natalie and I sat in her office in the back of the tutoring center, I began wondering if "ministry" might be a more everyday concept than I had previously imagined.

As we discussed the formidable demands of her work, Natalie paused and smiled at me, explaining, "You know, you can't define ministry by who signs your paycheck. Regardless of whether you work in a church setting or raise support as a missionary, if you are living for Christ, whatever you do is ministry." In the midst of the shouts of joy and mild mayhem of the tutoring center, my understanding of vocation and the nature of God's will began to deepen. I started to grasp the truth that while I might not be able to predict what projects or places God would lead me over the course of my life, or even during the next week, I could walk in the center of God's will *without* specific knowledge. As Paul writes in 1 Corinthians 10:31, "So, whether you eat or drink, or whatever you do, do everything for the glory of God." Through my conversation with Natalie, I came to believe that if I lived each day following this command—wanting to bring glory to God and further the kingdom of God— I would be living in the center of God's will regardless of what specific decisions I made.

As the summer unfolded, my understanding of vocation continued to develop: living in Durham's West End neighborhood slowly opened my eyes to the universality of Christian vocation. During a series of conversations with my housemates, who were also interning in Durham, Jesus's words in "The Lord's Prayer" came into focus. Jesus prays to God, "Your kingdom come. Your will be done, on earth as it is in heaven." For me, this prayer speaks to Christian vocation regardless of career path. Both in and out of the workplace, Christians can center their efforts on sharing the love of God in our complex and often painful world.

Jesus's prayer that we bring the kingdom of God to earth goes hand in hand with Paul's exhortation to "do all to the glory of God." The practice of simply being present with others and striving to live into our gifts allows us to become more fully the people that God created us to be and to bring the kingdom of heaven to earth. That summer, I saw the interns whom I lived with and the children whom I worked with bring the kingdom of God to earth in completely unique ways, sometimes through sharing a laugh or an insight and other times by offering a skill or service that only they were equipped to give at that particular moment. This vocational model of "being" and of living increasingly fully into one's unique giftedness has become the foundation of my understanding of Christian calling, a calling that encompasses all moments, actions, and encounters of the day.

Nevertheless, this conviction cannot stand alone as the only tool necessary to live a life of worship and prayerful discernment. For me, listening for God's voice in prayer and through the words and actions of others also contributes to the beautiful and difficult process of discernment. I try (and sometimes fail) to intentionally set aside time for prayer. In our noisy and frenetic world, I find it immensely helpful to seek out space to listen for God's voice, both in Christian community and in solitude.

Learning to seek out God's voice and to long for God's supernatural guiding hand lies at the heart of discernment. In his book *The Call*, Os Guinness stresses the importance of patience and faithfulness in the "mystery" of discerning calling. He cautions against the tendency to rush toward explicit and easily crystallized plans, quoting Oswald Chambers: "If you can tell where you got the call of God and all about it, I question whether you have ever had a call. . . . The realization of it in a man's life may come with a sudden thunder-clap or with a gradual dawning, but in whatever way it comes it comes with the undercurrent of the supernatural, something that cannot be put into words."[1]

As I press forward on the path of vocational discernment and continue to listen for the call of God, I hunger to develop an awareness of the mystery of God: that God's ways are not our ways, and as such, God's call on our lives may not be easy to articulate or easy to translate into practical terms.

Recently, at a seminary's admitted students day, a pastor reminded those gathered that we don't need to fully know or understand the "big picture" of our lives, we just need to seek the next step in our journey of discernment. This reminder has been an immense comfort to me. While I don't feel alone in my uncertainty around vocation—many of my friends are also unsure about what lies ahead for them after graduation—discernment feels more urgent now that I have a degree and I'm still not sure what I will do with it.

This fall, I moved across the United States to a new city and a new school. I know that I love theology and I love teaching young people, but I don't feel particularly drawn to parish ministry nor do I want to

---

1. Chambers, Oswald. *My Utmost for His Highest* (New York: Dodd, Mead & Company, 1935).

become an academic. While I'm still brainstorming ideas for what next steps I will take when I finish my theology degree, I am confident our mysterious God will surprise and bless me with his creative guidance.

In Romans 11:33, Paul writes, "O the depth of the riches and wisdom and knowledge of God! How unsearchable are his judgments and how inscrutable his ways!" I still feel far from a full understanding of calling and vocation, but I am no longer afraid that one misstep or foolish choice will throw me forever off the path that God will provide. God's ways may be beyond our knowing at times, but God is good and God is love. Because seeking to further the kingdom of God and walking in love are the universal vocations of the Christian life, each day I welcome the practice of trusting in the journey. The process of discernment rarely proves easy or straightforward, but as I strive to align my steps with Christ's, I've discerned a new way forward. As I seek always to move toward the center of God's will, I know it won't always be straightforward, but I now feel called to the journey of discovery one step at a time.

QUESTIONS FOR DISCUSSION:

1. Martinez's original plan to find her vocation included a focus on understanding herself. How can self-understanding support a search for one's calling? Has it helped for you?
2. This essay features several scripture passages. Do you think of particular scripture passages when you consider vocation? If so, which ones? If not, why not?

8

AN UNWILLING PILGRIM

An Angry Young Woman's Faith Journey in College

Anna DeWeese

Unexpected. This is how I describe my faith journey throughout college. After that, bolstered by the perspective of the past ten-plus years, another accurate word is: incredible. Looking back at those four years, it's also accurate to describe that time as a struggle—maybe even a fight. You know that teenager who looks forward to college because of all the freedom she will have to do whatever she wants and make her own choices, no longer held captive by the rules and boundaries of her youth? That was me, particularly in regard to my faith and religious practice. I entered college in what might have been the low point of my faith journey thus far, and I had no idea that my life could or would change in quite the way that it did. I struggled, a lot, and I didn't know whether the faith of my childhood would have much meaning to me as an emerging adult, or if I wanted it to have meaning in my adult life. But here I am, writing this now, grateful for the struggle.

My wrestling with faith actually started before I went to college and had been building throughout my teen years. Some of my earliest memories include events and experiences at the First United Methodist Church in Mena, Arkansas. Church was fun back then: vacation Bible school, children's music programs, sneaking into the high school Sunday school room to play on the bean bags while my parents were in Bible study.

My father answered a call to ministry when I was seven years old—too young to totally grasp how his new profession would change my life, but old enough to know that my life would definitely be changing. My family moved to Missouri in order for him to attend seminary at St. Paul School of Theology, and we moved back to Arkansas in 1994, where he was placed in his first appointment in the small, small town of Bearden. As a ten-year-old I was nervous to be the new kid in town and rather unsure what it meant to be the new preacher's kid, but we were welcomed by that congregation and the community, and my family was able to begin growing into our new lives as a pastor's family. Church was primarily fun then, too.

Without question, my father is incredible at his job and I am blessed to have him be both my parent and my pastor, but the difficulties of his profession have often trickled down into our family. I don't remember the first time I heard someone allude to the preacher's kid stereotype, but it was obvious that being a "PK" was a big deal. I eventually understood that being a PK has a lot to do with moral and social standards that others expect of you. Growing up, I often felt held to higher standards than other children. Feeling pressured by these PK standards (that I felt were flawed and unfair) often made life uncomfortable, and the discomfort only increased with age as my awareness of others' scrutiny expanded.

By the time I reached high school, after moving a couple of times, I no longer enjoyed going to church. Expected to sit in the right pew and keep a smile plastered on my face, attending church felt like a performance most of the time. An air of competition seemed to hover over the congregations my dad served, and a lot of stock was placed in how they compared themselves to other churches in town. I still had some fun during youth group events or working with the younger children's programs, but as I matured in high school, the majority of my church experiences were marked by a feeling of disillusionment. Why was I going to church—to worship and learn something or to put in an appearance?

These social pressures were exacerbated by racial dynamics in the towns we lived in, and I quickly learned that whom I chose to befriend was a problem. It was made clear to me in subtle and not-so-subtle ways that inviting certain people to church would not be appreciated, especially for the preacher's daughter. Living within communities with such stark racial and social standards, eleven o'clock on Sunday mornings was very much the most segregated hour in town each week. I came to see people who claimed to be upstanding, Christian citizens as hypocrites and bigots. It made no sense to me why someone's skin color or the part of town they lived in mattered so much when it came to church. I thought that the Gospels taught us to love and take care of one another, and that all are welcome in the Body of Christ. From my vantage point, however, I saw instead just how un-Christian the people in the pews could be—inhospitable, exclusivist, elitist, and intolerant. Having these same people teach me how to behave and believe felt confusing, frustrating, and angering. By the time I was preparing to go to college, I had had enough.

I left for Hendrix College excited for many things, but top of the list was no longer being required to go to church. I felt free! I relished the thought of no longer living under the standards and pressures associated with my father's profession. Finally, I could be who I wanted to be. Hendrix is a small liberal arts college in Arkansas that is affiliated with the Arkansas United Methodist Conference, but I chose to attend Hendrix for reasons other than its Methodist connections. Many members of the college staff knew that I was a Methodist PK, so I hadn't fully escaped, but I kept my distance. I had no desire to go to church or participate in church-related activities, campus ministry organizations, or faith-related student groups, and I didn't. For the first time in my eighteen years of life, going to church was optional and I savored staying away.

My choice deeply concerned my parents. While my parents worried about me, they also knew how unhappy I had been with faith and the Church throughout most of high school. I left for college barely holding on to my Christian roots, embittered toward all organized religion. For a time I tried on the "agnostic" label, but I never fully let go of my belief in a greater power in the universe—something that was still very true for me—a power that I felt and knew to be real and good but remained beyond human control. I couldn't totally give up God, but attending church felt like empty ritual. A middle ground seemed to emerge by not going to church and only talking about my belief in God when explicitly asked. I went to church when I traveled home on school breaks, but only to support my dad. Cynicism and a strong sense of distrust defined my attitude toward Christianity and religion and I didn't think they had anything left to offer me.

I had a desire to study and work with people, hopefully in a way that would help those who were struggling, and I decided to major in psychology to pursue a possible career in behavioral sciences. Because Hendrix is a liberal arts college, students are required to take courses across academic disciplines rather than more singularly focus on courses only within one's declared major. Wanting to get the humanities requirement out of the way quickly, in my freshman year I looked for a class to take in the Religion and Philosophy Department, and, for reasons I can't totally explain, I registered for a world religions class.

That introductory course on the world's religions had an indelible impact on my life. It turned my faith journey around, and my descent into total cynicism toward Christianity and religious practice began to shift. The professor designed the course so that the component on Christianity came last. Whatever reasoning he may have had for doing so, this pedagogical approach turned out to be very important to my faith journey. I entered the classroom on day one tired of Christianity, and only mildly interested in learning about other traditions. If Christianity had come first, I may have rejected it completely.

Showing us his earnest interest and respect for the world's wisdom traditions and their beliefs and practices, my professor impressed me greatly with his skill in introducing us to these varied traditions. He gave us much more than an intellectual exploration of the world's religions and created a space in the classroom for us to make more personal connections and meaning with what we learned. His manner of facilitating discussion encouraged a diversity of opinion while ensuring that we understood the basic tenets of the traditions we studied, including their histories and how followers practice them today. Hinduism, Buddhism, Judaism, Islam, Indigenous Traditions, all came alive and I was fascinated. Every couple of weeks, as we engaged in a new tradition, I found myself calling home to express my joy and excitement at discovering a new way of being and believing. I wanted to meditate, learn Hebrew, travel to the source of the Ganges, and hear the call to prayer. I loved talking about faiths and spiritual practices that seemed to offer so much more than the Christianity of my youth!

Several times, during these excited calls home, my father, patiently and respectfully listening to me, would offer a brief response, "Remember your roots." It must have been difficult to hear me speak so passionately about having found so much from traditions other than Christianity, all the while hoping and praying for my happiness and spiritual well being. I deeply admire my parents for giving me that space. By the end of the semester, my experiences engaging with other traditions had been much more than intellectual. I felt rejuvenated, hopeful that organized religion could be a source of spiritual growth and comfort. It was not all empty ritual carried out by those who cared more about how they looked performing those rituals than what any of it meant. By learning about other religions and systems of belief, the course had prepared me for contemplating my own.

Finally, the class moved to Christianity. Rather than treat the material with skepticism or indifference, I approached my tradition with ears to hear. I had found so much to appreciate within other traditions and moved beyond simple understandings and even false information I previously had of the complexities of other faiths and practices. The openness and acceptance I had developed toward other traditions and what they offered the world helped me realize that I could approach Christianity in a similar posture. I could be gentle with myself and relax in the tensions present in Christianity, unafraid of what I might find. I had a new set of tools and the strength to be a more direct agent of my spiritual formation and not feel trapped by the sociocultural context in which I had been raised. From there, my major and my life continued to change.

Looking back, I realize now that the experiences of my youth had left me heartbroken and college was the time I needed to heal my relationship with Christianity. All of the anger and confusion I felt toward the church came from a place of feeling betrayed. The messages of the gospels I had learned from the hundreds of sermons I listened to my father give growing up, came into conflict with the actions and attitudes of the people sitting next to me in the pews. Did I expect perfection? Of course not. But, I longed for a better vision of Christian living. It was not enough to "Love thy neighbor" only if they talk, dress, look, and act a particular way that we have decided is right.

I graduated from Hendrix with a degree in religion. While it was clear I did not feel called to seek ordination, I did seek further graduate theological studies for the sake of both my academic and spiritual growth. I went on to complete an MA in Systematic Theology from

Union Theological Seminary in New York City, and now I work with faith-based and contemplative organizations as an educator and program coordinator, seeking to expand the ways in which our beliefs and spiritual practices can bring about social change. In addition to my own work, I have many dear friends and colleagues who are working in religious and faith-based organizations of all kinds, providing powerful ministry to the communities they serve: pastors, rabbis, chaplains, teachers, writers, activists, musicians. I love having so many connections to different churches and faith-based networks that provide me a wealth of opportunities to experience and engage with the ways that faith can be expressed. I still have hang-ups about going to church and do not attend services regularly. But unlike the angry, hurt eighteen-year-old who left for college, I am comfortable with my spiritual identity and I have a deep appreciation for all of my experiences. My freshman self would be utterly amazed by who I have become.

My faith is grounded in the power and love of God and the embodied example of that love in Jesus. I seek to live my life in response to this love, in the relationships I have with other people and other spiritual traditions. Part of growing up is the transition from the innocence and simplicity of youth to a complex, nuanced existence shaped by forces and systems beyond our control. Essential to this process is the understanding that life requires making choices and learning how to deal with the impacts and outcomes of those choices. Having faith is similarly a choice, and it is a choice that we must consciously and actively make day after day. Our relationships, with other persons and with the Spirit, require active engagement in order for them to flourish. The world is a dynamic place, and if our faith is to sustain us we must live into it, rather than merely rest upon it. Struggling with one's faith is not a sign of failure or otherwise a negative aspect of one's character and being. To struggle, to have doubts, to say "no" when something feels wrong, to resist a practice or belief that harms rather than heals—these are all important experiences and qualities because they help us to make informed choices about how to be in the world.

My faith journey through college was most definitely a struggle but it is one I thank God that I had. My struggles with faith and church are not necessarily over, and I still grapple with what it means to me to claim a Christian identity. I continue to look within and beyond the Christian tradition for resources and practices to enrich my spirituality and inform my life. There may come a time when I am challenged so much that I again question the root of my faith and beliefs. If so, my hope is that my previous struggles will serve as a reminder that it is possible to make it through the night and into the dawn. I'm eager—even blessed—to see where the Spirit will guide me next.

QUESTIONS FOR DISCUSSION:

1. DeWeese credits her world religion class as important in growing her ability to appreciate religion again. Have you experienced classes that have accomplished similar aims? If not, why not?
2. How can struggle play a part in faith journeys? How can colleges and universities support students as they struggle?

Section III

Sex and Sexuality:
One Body, Many Members

Perhaps my favorite college class was taught by a United Church of Christ pastor turned family studies professor. The course: Human Sexuality. It was always full, so I had to wait until my senior year to take it. I've forgotten the details of most of the class lectures and sold the textbook long ago, but I do remember the professor's most common phrase: "Understanding sexuality is the most important component to understanding one's self." The essays in this section lend support for my professor's claim.

Steven Porter's essay "The Harm of Keeping Silent: Secret Romance on an Evangelical Campus" tells of the extreme lengths to which Porter went to negotiate dating on his college campus. In "Through the Grave: A Story of Transition and Resurrection" Andrew Leigh/Amanda LeAnn finds a faith community, loses it, then finds another. Agnes Potamian's essay, "As We Forgive Those Who Trespass against Us," which is both haunting and beautiful, reveals the horror of sexual violence and argues for a more engaged sexual ethic. While many have called for a more reflective, embodied faith, Michelle Johnson's essay, "Intertwining Cycles" describes her journey to claim one. Finally, in "Out of the Closet and Back to Church" Kyle J. Thorson writes of his unusual coming out, and his coming in to a Lutheran campus ministry at a large public university.

Self-understanding requires rich, multidimensional understanding. Is sexuality the most important part? It may be wise to take each case individually, but the essays in Section III show that, for many students, sexuality is a primary component without which all else is lost.

9

THE HARM OF KEEPING SILENT

Secret Romance on an Evangelical Campus

Steven Porter

I feel my pulse race as I knock on the apartment door this November evening. Meeting someone for the first time is always uncomfortable, but having never experienced anything quite like this curiously code-pendent anxiety and excitement, I'm left with no greeting to utter but a strained hi when the door opens. Standing in that second-floor apart-ment doorway is my date, a thin twenty-four-year-old politically minded sweetheart, smiling warmly. "Please, come in."

My stomach gnarls into a series of knots as the door closes behind me. I've been on a handful of dates in my years, but the insanity of planning one with someone I've just met—online, no less—is entirely new, equal parts terrifying and exhilarating. No one knows I've slipped out-of-town for the evening, let alone for a date. No friend or family member will be checking up on me or asking how it went. I'm on my own, responsible for my own well-being for once and with no idea what I'm doing.

Furthermore, I've balked at an offer to first meet publicly at a res-taurant for dinner, petrified as I am of being discovered in public with the stranger. What if I run into someone from church or school and their unavoidable questions? So whatever is to transpire between us this November evening will happen, I've decided, in the second-floor apartment out of town.

Not five steps onto the beige carpet, I freeze, wide eyes locked on the thing near the floor in the kitchen: a wine rack populated by several bottles. I've never had even a sip of alcohol and have no intention of breaking that streak, not this night. My inhibition must keep watch against threats to the innocence of this meeting, which is not sexual and must remain so. Keeping the bottles corked is now priority number one, though I admittedly possess no plan to keep the red and white at bay. I must remain sober, ready to flee at a moment's notice, excuse myself to my car, get back on the interstate and return to the security of my dorm room on the campus of my conservative evangelical university.

The drive had seemed to take days. I'm not sure what kept me from pulling a U-turn and heading back to the secure bubble administrators had so nobly afforded me, where the powers that be built spiritual reflection time into my class schedule and professors talked openly about the integration of Christianity and higher learning, where time alone with members of the opposite sex in residential areas was strictly regulated to a few hours per week with policies to keep doors open, lights on, feet grounded, and blankets for personal use only. Each inter-state mile marker I passed, however, had incrementally solidified my choice to steal away for the night. Looking back, oddly enough, I think my decision to follow through with the clandestine date had less to do with the person I was meeting than with the university I was leaving.

To be fair, I enjoyed campus life, generally speaking. I found people friendly enough and sincere in their religious and political views. They committed themselves to academic and extra-curricular interests, as college students should, and many of them devoted time and energy to lay ministry and Christian causes. By my sophomore year, however, I felt so philosophically out of place on campus that the administration's prized insular bubble—maintained with codified temperance policies alongside more damaging hallmarks of the Holiness movement—felt less like a refuge than a suffocating vacuum.

In an ironic blow to my spiritual wellbeing, I found the vacuum's negative atmospheric pressure most pronounced during mandatory three-times-weekly chapel services, which would migrate during my junior year to a brand new 3,800-seat, $22 million auditorium. While guest speakers spoke brilliantly on matters of social justice, personal piety, and church leadership, those who dared offer a sexuality-themed sermon rarely left me feeling anything but dirty and broken. Their messages were nothing new to me—I'd grown up hearing cautionary tale after sexually transmitted cautionary tale—but my newfound sophomore self-awareness turned the claims I'd once found satisfactory into increasingly intolerable fiction.

It's not that I was having sex. I started my sophomore year without having so much as a first kiss, let alone a first-time story. The thin layer of filth I sensed on my skin after so many of those compulsory chapel sermons was related first and foremost to the profound sense of otherness they perpetuated. Speakers either pretended students in my situation don't exist, or they flat out condemned the hypothetical identity I'd learned to deny with a poker face and topic change. Though I'd never acted on it, I'd for years experienced the chronic symptoms of a disorder the evangelical diagnostic manual labels *same-sex attraction.*

Long before I knew what it was, I knew it was wrong. I'd been taught since early childhood to view homosexuality as a monolithic perversion completely outside God's will for humanity. Even before I'd ever met or heard of a gay person, my grandmotherly first grade teacher went on an in-class diatribe against Hollywood's lionization of lesbian love. Without anyone in my life to debunk her slander, I went years hearing nothing but confirmation: gays are perverts, pedophiles, practitioners of bestiality. The moderate voices in my life taught that homosexuality is tantamount to alcoholism, a predisposition toward brokenness that Jesus died to mend. Accordingly, I told myself God only makes straight people, all of whom are bent on sin, some of whom are bent on the most unspeakable of sins.

This fear of falling prey to my own personal vice, in fact, contributed to my decision to attend the conservative university in my hometown. Even after graduating as valedictorian of my Christian high school and winning a full-ride scholarship to any college or university in the state, I didn't bother researching or touring the campuses of Indiana University, Purdue, Butler, DePauw, Rose-Hulman, or any other Indiana school. I feared their liberal environments would encourage me to embrace a gay identity. I settled instead, albeit halfheartedly, on an institution that would do the exact opposite: encourage me to embrace a very specific permutation of Christianity while denouncing my romantic longing as one of Satan's many lies.

Indiana Wesleyan University offered a beautiful campus, burgeoning Division of Communication, and refreshing honors college curriculum, plenty to convince me I wasn't drawn primarily by the perceived safe haven from my own degeneracy. So when I moved into my dorm with a midnight curfew, I was ready to immerse myself in campus life, to glean the most I could from the embodied learning traditional college campuses offer. Everything was new and fresh, challenging but rewarding, making freshman year perhaps the most enjoyable of the four.

I even warmed up to the idea of talking about homosexuality academically, an appealing way to externalize something that, even now, is difficult to discuss in first person. Serving as an unexpected primer on gay and lesbian liberation theology my first semester, I helped research and co-write a "white paper" concerning how Christian churches should respond to questions of sexuality. The section I wrote contained a mini-treatise explaining that the question of whether my attractions are hard-wired or acquired is inconsequential to my biblical mandate to avoid perversion. I wrote:

> Every postpubescent human being has innate sexual urges, so whether some people are born with homosexual tendencies is irrelevant. In the same way that a heterosexual man has a *natural* drive for premarital sex, it may very well be a *natural*—or at least an *innate*—drive for some to have homosexual relations. We must distinguish, though, between our innate selves and those temptations innate to ourselves.

Within a couple months of writing those words, however, such succinct academic responses to questions about my own innate sexual self seemed increasingly dishonest and paper-thin.

In what passed as rebellious my freshman year, several classmates and I decided to spend the night one weekend at our friend Sean's house off-campus, something against school rules for members of the opposite sex. Sean was openly gay, so policies forbidding mixed company sleepovers seemed a bit silly; regardless, when it came time to bunk down for the night, the girls sequestered themselves into a bedroom, leaving Sean and me to sleep on the living room floor.

By this point I'd developed a pretty strong crush on him, something I didn't admit until later. So when we lay on that hardwood floor, each in a fetal position with our feet pointed in opposite directions and our faces close enough to whisper without the girls hearing, Sean asked, "Are you sure you're straight?"

Groping for words, I hesitated then scolded myself for hesitating. I thought, "You've done this a million times: denial, poker face, topic change." I couldn't lie—he'd called my bluff before I'd even bet—but I couldn't tell the truth, either.

"Please don't ask me that," I whispered back, knowing my hesitation had already shouted a more nuanced response. Later on I wrote a poem about that moment comparing the position of our bodies to commas that put pauses places they don't belong. Publishing such poetry online (without annotation) gave me a false sense of intimate disclosure, a shallow catharsis when I felt I had nowhere better to decompress.

While I can't blame the emotional low points of my college career on the institution I elected to attend, I can say confidently that the expectations placed on me those four years added a lid atop the pressure cooker my equally conservative upbringing had spent years building around me. When the student handbook lists "homosexual behavior" in addition to "sexual misconduct" as a punishable offense, closeted students like me are left to wonder whether the policy is redundant or if holding hands with someone of the same sex might trigger disciplinary action. And when the underground of gays and allies on campus circulates stories of mandatory counseling for merely self-identifying as gay, there's a pretty big incentive to leave the pressure cooker lid undisturbed for as long as possible.

Rather than creating a community that promotes transparency and personal integration among all its members, the official stances taken by the university fostered a toxic culture for queer students like myself. Though individual classmates, faculty, and even some administrators were willing to speak without judgment about the possibility of being both gay and Christian, their hushed tones warned that repercussions await those who express such radical ideas. Some support beams had been installed—the diversity office and counseling center on campus sought to help queer students wade through the implications of their sexual orientations and gender identities—but the university failed to embrace these supports. And considering the fact that resident assistants were required to report possible student handbook violations to their superiors, I wasn't about to open up in my residence hall to disclose the tension I felt between my two identities. So I found myself floundering about the manicured campus with a secret struggle, unsure of whom I could trust to journey with me through that struggle. That's one reason I resorted to the Internet for likeminded fellowship. To be honest, I was somewhat surprised when I found what I was looking for.

Whereas some men see gay social networking sites as directories of potential sex partners, I found myself chatting with people like me who lived their real lives in unaccepting environments and sought freedom in the illusion of online privacy. Sure, there was a sexual overtone in some of these interactions, but I realize now that hiding behind my surface desire for arousal was a deeper desire for emotional intimacy, a romantic longing that chapel speakers overlooked when they spoke out against homosexuality.

A glimpse of that emotional intimacy prompted me to break character this November evening and meet the twenty-four-year-old out of town. Our online conversations had been entirely nonsexual, and I saw early on that we connected intellectually. After a few engaging conversations, he invited me to meet in person.

Society has caught up by now with the stranger dangers of Internet dating and provided plenty of stories to scare me away from the practice, so it had never been my intention to take things a step further. I still haven't made sense of precisely what gave me the gumption to quietly leave my dorm room and meet someone for my first gay date.

Driving down the interstate, I had plenty of time to think about what a stupid thing I was doing. But even the improbable headlines running through my head—*Homo predator kills Christian kid,* or *Golden boy caught gay-handed*—didn't convince me to stand him up, so I kept driving, secretly wishing that things would go terribly, that my date would be an asshole and that I could swear off gay men as sex-crazed and unworthy of my time.

As I drove down the interstate, I also thought back to the times I'd driven much farther to appease my gay curiosity. At the very end of my freshman year, Sean and a few other friends convinced me to go with them to a gay dance club. Since none of us were of drinking age, we had to drive two-and-a-half hours to an establishment out-of-state open to patrons eighteen and older. Since Sean was the only one with us who knew I was questioning my sexual orientation, I had to act like the novelty and camaraderie of the trip had been the main factors prompting me to go along. Instead of mingling openly or asking some guy to dance with me, I feigned heterosexuality, as I'd grown accustomed to doing, and I decided I'd just have to come back another time, alone.

So that summer, when I was working two jobs and living on campus, I took a gamble and relied on my 1997 Pontiac to make the five-hour round-trip trek to the gay club in Ohio. When I arrived, I was almost too nervous to go inside—I sat in the parking lot for probably fifteen minutes before I decided I'd come too far to simply turn around. I went in, forked over my cover charge and ID and let the staff mark black X's on my hands. Unfortunately, the nervousness I'd tried to leave in the car followed me inside, prohibiting me from striking up a conversation with anyone. I walked around, sat in the corner for awhile, and bought a Coke from the bar for $2.50, which I sipped while I stood on the border of the dance floor hoping someone would approach and ask me to join. No one did, so I got back in my car about two hours later and drove home, finally landing in bed at 5 a.m. after scrubbing my hands furiously until their black X's were mere shadows of the night before.

Feeling pretty dissatisfied in my shyness, I decided to return to the Buckeye State's gay establishment a couple weeks later—and then again a few weeks after that. I made a total of four solo trips that summer, all of them on Wednesday nights, the only evening I could steal away, thanks to my day job as a Christian radio DJ and night job waiting tables at Cracker Barrel. The midweek scene was surprisingly active, with swarms of college-age patrons of all sexual orientations together in one place. I was bolder in these subsequent visits, actually talking to people—and on two different occasions, attractive girls asked me to dance with them, so I did. Each of them wanted to bump and grind, so we did; and each of them noted that their talented gyrations failed to arouse a physical response from me, so they asked, in a shout barely audible on the dance floor, "Are you gay?"

Even among the clientele of a gay-friendly establishment out-of-state, I couldn't bring myself to respond in the affirmative—so I just shrugged, sending the girls off to find straight guys looking to grind. I later wrote an obtuse poem about the experience, publishing it online and even reciting it publicly once in another futile attempt at intimate disclosure. Even if I had been all alone on that dance floor in an empty building with the music cranked to ten, the sad reality is that at that point in my life I couldn't bring myself to tell anyone, "Yes, I'm gay," because I couldn't admit it to the man in the mirror—I couldn't make real and permanent something that was, in my mind, still so experimental.

Those four trips certainly acclimated me to the idea of driving by myself out of town to meet someone; they did not, however, prepare me for all that would transpire in the second floor apartment this November evening.

As the night wears on, my anxiety slowly dissipates. My date is a complete gentleman, proving just as engaging in person as he'd been online. We talk for hours into the night and watch an ungodly amount of *So You Think You Can Dance*, as he maintains a demeanor that is friendly but not the least bit threatening or overtly sensual. We're seated on opposite ends of his couch, but I decide it would be desirable to establish some sort of physical contact. Yawning to put my arm around him seems unreasonable, and the occasional touch of his knee goes unnoticed. So I muster the courage to make a move on him: reaching out my right hand with index finger extended, I poke him on the left shoulder, holding it there for a moment. He responds with a quizzical look and half-chuckle. (No one has ever accused me of being smooth.)

The flirtation escalates, little by little, until we wind up horizontal on the couch, my face very near his—I decide to kiss him.

Recalling the directions I learned from some movie, I move in ninety percent of the way and pause for him to close the distance—he doesn't, but he doesn't recoil, so I close the gap and kiss him on the lips. He kisses me back. We keep kissing for some time, in fact, and find ourselves making out for the next couple of hours—no sex, just kissing.

Whereas I'd hoped the twenty-four year old, undoubtedly more experienced than I, would push for something I didn't want so I could push back and be justified in my wholesale dismissal of gay men, he provides no such justification. Instead, he personifies the quirky, caring nonjudgmental conversationalist I yearn to know on an intimate level. He gives me the impression that our conversation could broach any topic with no risk of my secrets leaving his apartment. He takes interest in my life rather than peering voyeuristically at its parts. He wants to get to know me, just as I long to get to know him.

I return to my dorm room in the next morning's wee hours and fail to catch up on the sleep I missed the night before. I crawl onto the top bunk and face the wall to bawl as quietly as I can.

Reporting to work at Cracker Barrel the afternoon after my first kiss, I'm a wreck. My coworkers surely think this teetotaling college student just earned his first hangover, but the root cause of my pounding headache and despondency is not alcohol, but cognitive dissonance. I've made real what had, up until now, been hypothetical.

Not only do I feel as though there's nowhere I can go to decompress, but now I also feel as though there's no going back. I've crossed *the* line. Sure, I can still date girls, but at some point in any subsequent opposite sex relationship I'll have to disclose the curiosity of last night. I can gloss over the uneventful stories at the gay club and at Sean's house, but I can't sweep kisses under the rug so easily.

Despite the havoc my out-of-town date has wreaked on my emotional life, I decide to go back—twice. We still don't have sex, and he still provides the inviting sense of intimacy I've longed for. But after our third date I can't stand the duplicitous living any longer, so I cut ties with him, saying I have to go be straight because that's what God demands.

I cry again because I know I've hurt him (but I won't realize how injurious the "God card" can be until someone plays it on me a couple years later). It's not easy to hear someone you've developed romantic feelings for say that your feelings, though reciprocated, are sinful.

During my junior and senior years, I begin to scrutinize a long list of formerly unquestionable truth claims, one of them the notion that homosexuality falls unambiguously outside Christian orthodoxy. Instead of conforming idealistically to the only relational archetype conservative believers see in Scripture, I begin to think inductively, asking what it looks like to pursue human wholeness in light of the gospel. I acknowledge my own brokenness but refuse to believe that it prevents me altogether from perceiving even a shred of reality.

Knowing that experience is one of the four things John Wesley's quadrilateral identifies as the bases for solid theological conclusions, I realize that my romantic longing is absolutely relevant to questions about the intersection of morality and sexuality. I can't rely on Scripture or tradition alone; I have to incorporate experience and reason as well. And my experience leads me to believe that same-sex romance can be rightly subjugated to a love for God and that even two men or two women can participate in matrimony that reflects the trinity's unity in diversity.

While I still can't deliver a perfectly compelling argument to defend the idea that same-sex love is God ordained, I now fully believe that Scripture isn't as clear on the issue as the majority of evangelicals I've met would have me think. Accordingly, I begin to express these opinions my senior year, wrestling silently with their personal implications.

At the prompting of my closest friends, I cave and sign up my final semester for the free counseling services provided by the school. During the first of our weekly meetings I double-check to ensure that they won't refer me to reparative therapy or the school's disciplinary channels. Satisfied by their promise of confidentiality, I proceed to decompress. The process proves cathartic, so I begin looking for other avenues of intimate disclosure, not in some severed-limb of a gay identity expressed in secret, but among the people who know me as a whole person. I start coming out to friends on a regular basis and eventually muster the gall to tell my only sister that I believe it's possible to be a gay Christian. As unsettling as the disclosures have been, the resulting integration has been a worthwhile and healing process.

I sit my parents down with a pit in my stomach, now three years after my first kiss. I pull a one-page letter out of my pocket, and I read it aloud. The introduction to that, the most difficult letter I've ever written, sums up the unsettled lesson I learned about myself in my four years on the campus just across town from my parents' house: "There's no easy way to break news that you don't want to hear, and no matter which words I choose, you're not going to like what I'm about to say," I wrote. "But sometimes the harm caused by keeping silent outweighs the harm of speaking truth."

QUESTIONS FOR DISCUSSION:

1. For Porter, secrecy played a large part of his experience of sexuality in college. What about sex and sexuality should remain secret and confidential? What can colleges do to make space for those who want to share?

2. Many of this book's essays address college students' significant change from their first year to senior year. Porter's is no exception. Is such drastic change a necessary and important part of college life?

3. How can colleges and universities welcome students of all sexual orientations and identities? How does this question look different at religiously affiliated colleges?

10

THROUGH THE GRAVE

A Story of Transition and Resurrection

Andrew Leigh/Amanda LeAnn Bullard

A NEW LIFE

Sixteen years ago a call echoed through the congregation: "Is there anyone here who would like to give their life to Christ?" A young girl stepped forward. Escorted by her father, she wore a green and white dress. The pastor introduced her with the acknowledgment that she has been persistent in asking about baptism. When asked if she believed that Jesus Christ is her Lord and Savior her loud YES echoed through the room, raising chuckles from the congregation. Led to the baptismal pool, her head was barely visible as she met the pastor and was submerged three times, rising a new creature. Swept away by the Spirit, lost in the innocence of belief, that child could never imagine the path that day had set them on.

My childhood was full of church activities. Summers were filled with vacation Bible school and church camp. During the year I attended Sunday school and youth group, often in addition to other faith-based groups such as Bible Bowl. I possessed a knack for memorizing Scripture and excelled in activities designed to test biblical knowledge. In many ways I was the ideal Christian youth, attending conferences, completing mission trips abroad, and reciting entire books of the Bible from memory.

Church became my refuge from a world where it became increasingly obvious I didn't belong. Even in grade school I was bullied. Peers turned my name, Amanda, into an insult as kids called out, "It's a man, duh!" Their words struck deep within me, burying who I was beneath their hatred. I reacted poorly. Aggression became my defense as I fought back. Blamed for the conflicts that surrounded me, and instructed to conform, I was handed over to mental health professionals. Their medications made my life worse. Only my family and those at church put up with my eccentricities and breakdowns. I lived in constant fear of when the next crisis would happen, knowing I was fast approaching the limit of what I could survive.

DEATH

Church leaders noticed my alienation and lack of social skills and offered to help by taking me clothes shopping and emphasizing female traits. While I longed to roughhouse with the boys, I was always redirected "for my safety." My inquisitiveness began to create other barriers as I found I couldn't accept a literal interpretation of Scripture. Uneasy as I was, I stayed active as I knew that I had no friends outside of that congregation. Each night I prayed fervently that God would "make me normal" so I could be like the other kids. It would take years before I could embrace the fact that I *was* normal, years to realize that it was the church, society, and those around me who created an abomination by forcing me to deny who I was.

Everything that I tried to ignore came together the summer I turned fourteen. At a conference out of town, the girls in the youth group decided they were going to help me fit in. Their "cure" was a makeover. Over the course of hours my hair was straightened, makeup applied and I was instructed to wear one of the few dresses I owned. By the end of their ministrations I was unrecognizable, except for the deep sadness that still reflected through my brown eyes. As we walked to evening worship I felt I couldn't be more wrong, and I hated myself for not being who I was supposed to be—that is to say, who they expected me to be.

That night I learned how God can step into the most unlikely of situations. As we danced to blaring Christian rock I found myself carried away, lost in the music. In that moment I saw in my mind a woman in armor riding a warhorse. The sun shone, a pennant fluttering in the breeze above her as the wind rustled the grass. As I surveyed the scene a voice echoed through me. It was so strong that I not only heard it, but felt it reverberating through every fiber of my being. That voice promised that I was chosen for something special and that I would have a battle to fight. Shaken by the encounter, I turned to the youth pastor. Nothing in our church's teaching prepared me for that moment when God answered my prayers, but the pastor's response was devastating. "You are plagued by demons and need to pray harder" is a terrible message for anyone to hear, but for a fourteen-year-old it is enough to destroy your world.

With that event all the things I had done and believed fell to pieces. I could no longer accept the "truths" that I had learned growing up and I left the Christian faith. I left everything behind: my faith, moral guidance, support, and friends. Rejecting the pastor's assessment of demonic possession, I decided to believe the psychologists. My contact with God was reduced to a hallucination, and I ceased to believe. To survive, I convinced myself that I hadn't needed those things I abandoned. That day the brightness of the pure faith I'd had as a child was laid to rest. I resigned my soul to abandonment in a grave formed from misconceptions, barriers, and isolation.

THE WALKING DEAD

The problems in my secular life did not disappear after I left the church. In fact, they intensified. A high school dropout with a GED, I moved into my college dorm room at sixteen as I tried to flee from my parents' divorce, the isolation of high school, and years of having my emotions medically suppressed. Additionally, I still didn't know I could exist, or even that I might have a place in this world. From the outside, college appeared to solve every problem. I excelled academically, was nominally involved in student organizations, and worked a steady job. Internally, I stayed broken—not just spiritually but completely. I hated my body, and eventually turned to self-injury. A workaholic, my teachers praised my accomplishments while I hid how often I wanted to die.

Directed to the campus Gay Straight Alliance by the counseling center, who thought part of my troubles stemmed from a nonheterosexual orientation, I found a group that could understand my hatred of religion. With them, I questioned my sexuality, and later my gender identity. It was also in that community that I learned to view "Christians" as a threat. The "Christian" presence was everywhere, declaring us "perverse" or "abominations" and passing legislation that forces us to be less than those around us. Hate found a home in me as I found it easier and easier to curse those of faith, supported by the antagonistic community that offered me the first space I found to be myself.

In 2007, before I turned eighteen, I took a leave of absence from campus to study abroad. Isolated from even the small network of support I had built at school, I deteriorated. I first turned to alcohol—and upon realizing a growing dependence—to self-injury to avoid alcoholism. Self-injury started slowly, picking scabs from accidental injuries, but quickly exploded beyond what I could handle. I cut, burned, and salted my wounds. As I sank deeper and deeper into that hole, I lost my ability to cry. My only emotion was pain that strangled me even as it was the only thing that held me to life.

Looking back, even in the pit of that despair, God's hand was in my life. While in Spain, I would often walk through the Catedral de Murcia, a Roman Catholic cathedral. Though I would never consider attending mass there, the holy space gave me calm. The building challenged my assumptions of God and Christians. I marveled at the intricate structure, from the rising towers and ancient carvings of the exterior, to the gothic interior, with its dimly lit chapels and candle-lined recesses. As my hand drifted upon the cool, implacable stone I couldn't help but consider that a God who could inspire such a beautiful building couldn't be all bad.

Those peaceful walks were unable to contain the chaos that threatened to tear me apart. I returned home more broken than before. Suicidal ideation dominated my thoughts during the day. I started to cut even without an emotional trigger. I also discovered how oblivious the world can be to a person's pain. At the depths of despair I was cutting in class, and no one said anything to me about it.

God revealed a different way for me a few months later, in a manner indirect enough that I could accept it. While I wrestled with this mass of pain, emotions, and addiction I walked in the woods one spring day.

As I followed the winding trail I realized that, if I didn't come back, it'd be over a week before anyone would realize I was gone. I had my pocket knife with me, and as I passed the overgrown paths I thought about all the reasons why it wouldn't matter if I were dead. In the distance I saw an old bridge piling overlooking a river. It was just off the trail, close enough that I'd be discovered and far enough that I wouldn't be interrupted. My knife was in my hand as I watched the rushing water. As I thought about everything I couldn't handle I accepted that I wanted to be dead.

Then, up in the branches above me, a bird cried out. Its cheery song was a ray of light contrasting with the bitter darkness that held me. I gripped the knife tightly, feeling the cold edge resting on my wrist but as I listened to the birdsong I knew—deep down I knew—that I couldn't do it. I dropped the knife as I wept. Those bitter tears were sweeter than water in a desert. For a rare instant I felt something besides pain and isolation.

ROLLING BACK THE STONE

Healing is a long process. A dam had broken in me that day in the woods, but it would take long months to clear away the rubble to reveal the person trapped beneath. Through the support of new friends who held me through the nights, I moved ever so slowly toward health. My friends gave me the strength to reach out to some amazing mental health professionals. These counselors accepted me for who I was. Then, with their help, I was able to free myself from the burden of previous diagnoses.

Finally freed from seeing myself as mentally ill, I reconsidered what it meant to be myself. Soon thereafter, I spoke with a conference presenter about transgendered individuals, and without thinking these words spilled from my mouth, "I'd do it" I said, thinking of transitioning from female to male, "if I didn't think it would mean giving up on a law enforcement career." The presenter looked at me oddly and stated there was no reason transitioning would mean that I couldn't be a cop. Shaken, both by what I had said and the feelings her response had raised, I fled. Crying alone that night, I tried to rebury what I had just learned. I was frantic; all I knew about being transgender was that it would lead to discrimination, pain, and ultimately an untimely death.

Two days later I shared this event with a close friend. I tried to fight back the tears that fell unbidden, forgetting for a time how long I had sought their release. Gently my friend placed a hand on my knee and whispered words of power, words of rebirth. "It's OK if you're a boy." Tears flowed freely as I opened myself up, accepting that possibility. With that permission I found the barriers of my own internal oppression falling to pieces, revealing another life standing uncertainly at the entrance of the tomb that had held me captive my entire adult life.

AT THE ENTRANCE TO THE TOMB

Transitioning in the Midwest was not easy. Each new step required a major fight. I argued with doctors, administrators, and family as I tried to come out and claim my identity. I found Andrew Leigh was a perfect fit for the name I needed. A rearrangement of my birth middle name LeAnn, the name Andrew spoke to a masculine strength of a warrior who could face the challenges transitioning would create. Leigh, Old English for meadow, reflected the part of me that was nourished by sitting still outside. In the space of a year Amanda fell away as Andrew was revealed. I started testosterone, changed my gender marker on my driver's license and passport, and came out over and over again. The changes were drastic as those around me rejoiced in my newfound comfort with who I was. For the first time I could remember I was truly happy.

Being transgender is an awkward thing for someone of faith. Despite my previous rejection of religion, I did think about God. Specifically I wondered how God could make a mistake with me, putting a boy in a girl's body. With time, as I grew into my transition I realized the truth. No mistake was made in making me who I am. My gender is a part of the journey I've been given, one that is remarkably beautiful when seen in its entirety. Obsessed with discomfort, I initially missed the miracle of emerging as who I am. As I accepted God's role in making me transgender, I realized that I lacked a faith tradition.

As I recognized this need I tried to fill in the gaps with pagan spirituality. I used rune casting, wind, and prayers to the sun to reach for the

Divine that had been so close to me as a child. God's creation—sunsets and hills, solemn walks through the forest, and the waves of the sea—replaced God in my life. These practices kept me going but were not satisfying as creation is but a pale imitation of the love offered by the Creator.

As Christmas approached, I found myself besieged by the hoard of emotions that holidays conjure. Ever since my parents' divorce around Christmas I'd struggled with the holiday as it reminded me of happier times that would never be. While processing those emotions I found a longing to return to church. My longing was not for God who I had abandoned long ago. I knew that, being openly transgender and pansexual, I could expect no welcome at most churches. It was the Christmas carols of my youth that eventually drew me in. I missed singing them and so I decided to attend the Christmas Eve service at the church I had attended in high school.

Christmas Eve came and passed. An unplanned family discussion about pronoun use and my transition ran late, and church had been forgotten. But 2011 was a special year, as Christmas fell on a Sunday. Realizing that the songs would probably include some of my favorites, I woke up early on Christmas day and did the extraordinary: I went to church. I had prepared for hostility because I presented as male and was shocked to discover that I was ignored. Shaken by this lack of reaction I sat in the back of the congregation, waiting uncertainly for something I couldn't describe.

Something did happen, despite the lack of effort from the congregation I had once called my own. As we sang "Silent Night," I felt a presence that I had long forgotten. A warmth that encouraged me filled my body, overwhelming my senses and stirring the neglected spirit, the core of myself that I had long abandoned for dead. As the service concluded I realized that what was still missing in my life was spirituality. I believe a person is made of three parts, mind, body and spirit that together form the self. By transitioning I had reconciled my mind and body, but until that moment my spirit had lay untouched, still as a corpse in a tomb.

RESURRECTION

My experience of Christmas lingered with me, and as I reflected on my goals for 2012, I decided to add "revisit being around the Christian faith." At the time I thought I'd attend a local church once or twice, improve my tolerance for Christians and be done with it. God had other plans for me, however.

I chose the specific church for two reasons. First, I had heard the name mentioned by two people I worked with who were allies and had supported me during my transition. Second, I saw their welcome statement included sexual orientation. I knew that was no guarantee of acceptance of someone like me, but it meant this parish, which happened to be Episcopalian, would be as likely a place to tolerate me as any.

So I showed up, and my first week proved to be one that would shape the coming year and redefine my life entirely. Baptismal Sunday, celebrated on the first Sunday after Epiphany, was the first time I visited the Episcopal Church. The contrast between their tradition and what I had been raised with became apparent instantly in the simplest way: I was welcomed. From the minute I entered the nave I was greeted cheerfully. As I flipped through the bulletin, a stranger approached and offered to help me follow the service. During my entire time there, it was made clear that they wanted to invite me to be a part of their community.

The welcome I received was accentuated by the sermon. As befits Baptismal Sunday, the priest spoke of the lifelong nature of baptism. While reflecting on his words, I found myself opening my past and seeing how the decision I made as a young girl to give herself over to Christ had shaped the young man I had become. I realized that the reason I was there, at that church, at that moment, was that I needed to relearn how I could live out my baptism as the person I had grown up to be.

The week continued when on Wednesday I found myself returning to that odd place for their college meal. I made a point of outing myself over dinner, as I'd decided to face the reality that I wouldn't be fully welcome early. I was astounded by how much of a nonissue my identity was. Even after knowing I was trans, they still wanted to talk to me. Their acceptance was so unexpected that I didn't know what to make of it. This family-sized parish, in a small Midwestern town was not only tolerant of a trans° pansexual, but loving, inviting, and respectful, surpassing all of my expectations![1]

That Saturday I arrived for the choir practice I'd seen advertised on the bulletin board. As music has always played a part in my spiritual life, I felt that choir might be a good way to learn more about this church. Once again I was welcomed without question, and before the end of my first week a cassock and cotta had been found for me. Thus by my second Sunday I was processing with the choir to the front of the church, understanding little of the service, but knowing that somehow I belonged.

That first week set the tone for the following year. As time passed the liturgical customs and Anglican traditions became less strange, and then comfortably familiar. I grew to love the service and even more the community who became friends, then family. Fascinated by every aspect of church life, I found myself president of the campus organization, on the parish life committee, volunteering with the food service program, and serving in the liturgy. I started to attend diocesan events, and then General Convention 2012, where I watched in amazement as the national church affirmed my place in Christ's body by adding gender identity and expression to the nondiscrimination canons.

As I grew in my faith, and began to see how Jesus's resurrection had led to my own rebirth into the St. Andrew's community, I was again challenged by the direct presence of God. Unlike before, our local priest was prepared for my questions. Introduced to prayers of adoration, I found that what I had once taken for insanity was a precious gift, to be nourished and guided within a loving community. My hectic schedule, the remains of my workaholic self, took on a relaxing quality with the addition of daily prayer. The future I had planned for myself, involving a career in law enforcement and librarianship, fell to pieces as my perception of my life changed. Yet the loss did not shake me for long as I found myself drawn toward vocational discernment with the Episcopal Service Corps, an organization in which young adults serve, worship, listen, and reflect on where we see Jesus in our lives. Through Jesus's love shown to me by the St. Andrew's community I have been

---

1. I am using *trans°* to refer to the continuum of individuals whose gender identity and expression, to varying degrees, does not correspond to their assigned sex. I use *pansexual* to refer to a sexual orientation characterized by the potential for aesthetic attraction and/or sexual desire towards people of any gender or sex.

guided to a new life, fully resurrected as my mind, body, and soul were united by the power and love of the Triune God.

ENTERING THE SUNRISE

On Ash Wednesday 2012 I found myself meditating alone in the columbarium behind the church. The sun was shining on an unseasonably warm day, perfect for sitting outside. As I sat peacefully, a prayer emerged from within. Not a list of praise or complaints, but a simple contentment to be in the presence of the God who surrounded me. This intimacy was in many ways deeper than my prior feeble attempts at prayer. Within those brick walls I once again heard God speaking to me directly. This voice did not forcibly reverberate through my body, but was soft and gentle, a whisper on the wind calling to the innocent belief of long ago. This presence called me by name, a name that I had never heard before. In the silence and the breeze I heard "Amanda AND Andrew" said together, overlapping and harmonizing, and for the briefest instant I knew how who I am involves both names coexisting.

True to my earlier patterns of postponing self-discovery, I initially resisted this discovery about myself. But as the year turned I again began to chafe under the burdens of a binary identity. I resisted checking the "male" box on forms, not because I didn't see myself as a man, but because I hated the realization that checking one box was a denial of the other. I again struggled with how to acknowledge a gender that society told me did not exist.

Unlike before, I was surrounded by people and an environment that could help me discover who I was. It was while I was on staff at a youth event that I came to understand the underlying problem. The answer came, as it often has for me, through music. As we sang "Prince of Peace" I found myself shifting from the male part on the chorus to the female part on the verses and found that it was then that I was complete. In that instant I knew that who I was involved being both a man and a woman simultaneously.

The following weekend I sought the encouragement of other peer ministers and our campus missioner. They were there for me, supporting my identity, my name, and offering to help me find a way to attend to express my new understanding. With their support, and the blessing of my parish family I finally came out as bigender, both male and female, both Amanda and Andrew, a beautiful part of God's creation. As the God who made night and day also made the liminal, colorful periods of dawn and dusk, so too have I been made. I have been blessed with an opportunity beyond my wildest dreams as a child. My prayers to be "normal" have been answered with gifts that are beyond anything I could have asked for. I now live openly as I was meant to, supported by my parish and church family, reflecting God's glory through my actions, words, and song.

QUESTIONS FOR DISCUSSION:

1. The essay addresses the theme of acceptance in several ways—in community, of one's self and sexuality, in baptism. What aspect of Andrew Leigh/Amanda LeAnn's story of acceptance (and rejection) was most powerful for you?

2. Andrew Leigh/Amanda LeAnn describes several direct experiences of hearing God's voice in prayer. Have you or someone you have known ever had a similar experience?

3. What might institutions like the church learn from Andrew Leigh/Amanda LeAnn's story?

11

AS WE FORGIVE THOSE WHO TRESPASS AGAINST US

Agnes Potamian

I was baptized in the Episcopal Church, a denomination that hails itself as open and welcoming. I grew up with a deep sense that I was always good enough and always welcomed at the altar table, that God unfathomably loved me, and that I was a part of the Body. But during my sophomore year at a small liberal arts college, I found myself squirming in my pew. My loving, compassionate friends from my campus ministry surrounded me in the congregation, singing and praying and giving bear hugs at the Peace, but I found myself feeling too dirty to be there.

I felt completely isolated from the world swirling around me. The organ's chords blurred together into a ringing dissonance between my ears, humming amidst my frantic thoughts. I desperately prayed that I would not suck the person next to me into the black hole I felt like I was in. My lips instinctively recited the liturgy, but I felt as though I couldn't speak. I stood in my Sunday best, feeling like at any moment I would collapse into a quivering heap on the ground. This isn't where my college faith story begins, but this moment, as I slunk down behind the high walls of the old pews in my church one autumnal Sunday, was certainly the turning point.

I began my freshman year of college with a boyfriend, like many students do. For most freshmen, their high school relationships soon break off, as they find the demands of a long-distance relationship no longer outweigh the benefits. My relationship was different.

We had met at a youth leadership conference in Georgia. I was from Colorado, and he was from a town not far from where the conference was held. We exchanged phone numbers and the relationship blossomed by way of postcards and phone calls after I touched down in Denver. He was the first guy I dated who was also a Christian—a very different kind of Christian, but at least the kind of guy who said he would be happy to attend my church when he visited, and who wanted me to go to his. He came to my Episcopal Church, but did not understand the liturgy. He came from a Pentecostal background. My congregation's monotonous unison responses perplexed him.

I visited his church and was enamored with the eyes-closed, swaying type of worship, but still felt very cautious. That kind of worship was unnatural for me, but I tried it with an open mind. I was excited to finally see people my age in a church, not to be among the few under the age of sixty-five. Later that night, we went to an International House of Prayer meeting, and I experienced what I called the Holy Spirit. I met my boyfriend's good friend who claimed to be prophetic. He had reportedly seen a glimpse of the throne room, the room in heaven where God sits in His glory being praised day and night by cherubim and seraphim. This friend somehow possessed the ability to see angels and demons walking around our world like the ghosts from *The Sixth Sense*. When I met him, he prayed over me and I dreamed that angels he had seen in the room came and surgically removed a burned crust from my heart. It was powerful.

In hindsight, I still don't know if I believe the things I saw there. I do know I have never felt them again. At the time, I was completely hooked. As I dove into this new spirit world with my boyfriend, we worshipped and prayed together. We studied the Bible *together*. That was when the problems started. I took my newly found fervor and my deep-seated appreciation for the Episcopal tradition and discerned that I may have a call to ordained ministry. At the time I had just declared a religious studies major at my university, and was learning about the many ways one can interpret Scripture, especially through historical-critical lenses. My boyfriend was a strict, self-proclaimed literalist. To him every text was black and white while I preferred readings with shades of gray.

I was shy when I entered college, very uneasy and often quite afraid to stand up for myself, despite my quick wit, sharp tongue, and chronic extroversion. I called my boyfriend the second I could articulate what I was feeling: "I feel called to be a priest for God!" He replied that we all were. "No, I don't think you understand, I want to go to seminary and be a pastor." He told me women were not allowed to teach men. We began arguing. Often.

We argued with nearly every phone call. He told me women were supposed to be submissive to men, that he was told by God himself that I had been given to him to be his wife someday, to have, to hold, and to lord over forever. He illustrated dreams of travelling the world as missionaries, him teaching and me, obedient and submissive, following along bearing him children, wearing mostly the clothes he likes best. This went on for over a year. My mind has a great way of blocking painful memories, so I don't remember exactly how I got to where I ended.

My best friend and roommate finally started talking to me about my relationship. She told me she was concerned, that she thought my relationship was becoming emotionally abusive. I talked to my priest and told him what had been happening. He agreed. I decided to break up with my boyfriend. I had felt trapped for too long.

I called him up one evening and told him we were done. He simply responded, "No." I was so shocked that I ultimately agreed and hung up, still dating him. These calls went on for a week. I would muster up some small amount of courage only to find myself trapped under his ruling thumb, and having no memory of how I had let it happen. I finally sent him an email that I wrote while three of my closest friends sat in the room, hugging me, helping me form the words, and assuring me that I was safe. The next day I got a text from a mutual friend asking why my boyfriend wanted to stay at his place when coming to visit. But he wasn't scheduled to visit. I was terrified of the prospect since our final phone conversations made me think that he was not beyond violence. That night, I locked my dorm door for the first time all year and didn't sleep much, cowering in my bed. I told my mom, who then admitted to me that she had also once been in an abusive relationship. She called his mom, and his mom ensured that he did not come.

With that chapter of my life *finally* slammed shut, I found myself a blank page with hardly a sense of identity apart from him. For two years, I had built my entire concept of self around him. Apart, who was I? My once-strict life suddenly did not have imposed limits. I had partied in secret when I was dating my ex. It is clear to me now that I drank to try to forget him, to experience a few fleeting hours of freedom and autonomy. The first few times I just flirted with other guys, but the week before I broke up with him I actually cheated on him. How does a good Christian girl wearing a purity ring end up cheating on her boy-friend, drunk and in a bed that belonged to neither consenting person?

I began to party more. Harder. I hooked up with strings of guys, usually the ones who were far too good at manipulating me. I won attention by being the girl at the party in jeans and a t-shirt, a stark contrast to the glittering mini-skirts and heels so high your ankles shake when you walk. Instead of twittering and giggling in the center of the room, I fired off snarky comments in the corner and talked about theol-ogy. I thought I was doing some sort of ministerial thing, drinking and talking about God, somehow trying to show that not all Christians were stiffs.

I blacked out a couple of times. The last time I blacked out was soon before a law was passed banning the original formulation of Four Loko, an alcoholic energy drink with significant amounts of caffeine. I showed up at one of my good friend's frat houses, already three sheets to the wind. The last thing I remember clearly is sharing some of his Four Loko out of a glowing cup I had carried with me from an earlier glow stick party. The small amount of liquid in the cup never seemed to diminish, but glowed and replenished itself with every sip. I have only snapshot memories of being in the frat house laundry room with a rugby guy I'd made out with before. He was a known player. I was naked and on top of him.

Snapshot: I think I threw up either on him or next to him.

Snapshot: me, lying naked and alone in the laundry room. I put on the few clothes of mine that I could find.

Snapshot: running into two fraternity brothers upstairs. I think I was in just my bra and jean shorts. They got me a hoodie and sandals. I apologized profusely on the way home. I don't know how I got into my room; I had left my ID card behind. I woke up the next morning at 6 a.m. with the worst hangover I've ever experienced.

I received texts from my good friend asking if I was OK. Where was I? Was I hurt? He visited me later in the afternoon carrying a bag of my leftover clothes, my ID card, and Gatorade. He told me that his frat brother had told him what happened. I don't remember what my friend asked or told me next, but I remember somehow insinuating that I wasn't going to press charges. In my mind, it must have somehow been my fault. After all, I had been promiscuous lately, and maybe that was just what I got? Maybe I had consented and just don't remember. I got a text from the rugger later: "Thnx for being cool abt this."

I did not go to church the next day, and my Sunday attendance became sporadic. Before this experience, I had caught the rugger mixing drinks, but he didn't put alcohol in one of them. He meant to give me the alcoholic one, but switched them by accident. That night that I found myself in the laundry room was just the cherry on top, the confirmation that this guy was no good. Christianity taught me a radical sense of kindness and compassion, so we still cordially say "hello" when I see him, which is more often than I care to handle in such a small town.

Some time later, I can no longer remember when, one of the other rugby players asked me to dinner. We had mutual friends in ROTC, and he said he wanted to get to know me. He took me out to a nice dinner, picked me up and dropped me back off, and gave me a nice kiss at the end of the night. It wasn't the best date, and he wasn't as charming as I think he perceived himself, but I was content with the small miracle of normalcy I was finally experiencing. He brought me coffee in the library a couple of times that following week, and asked me on another date the following weekend. The plan was to have dinner and a movie at his apartment. I arrived and found out that the movie he had planned was *Piranha*, an awful, B-list, sci-fi, horror movie. I started to feel uncomfortable being there for some reason, but because the house was far off-campus, I couldn't leave. It felt like a fish when the water is starting to freeze over, swimming slower and slower. Within five minutes of the movie starting, he was forcefully putting his arm around me, pulling my face to him, trying to kiss me too hard. I tried to pull away several times, said that I wanted to watch the movie. He wouldn't let me. We had sex. I did not have much of an option. I left before it was really over and I think the only reason he let me is because he was disappointed. He drunk-called me a month later and told me that he had called another girl over just after I left, to finish.

That following Sunday, I went to church. Through the big church windows, I could see the big orange autumnal leaves spiraling downward out of the trees. The organ chords hummed their melodies and I kept from completely collapsing by focusing on the leaves outside of the window. During the Eucharist, we prayed,

> "Our Father, who art in heaven," and the images rolled through my mind like a bad movie. The drinks, the couches, the piranha, my friend's room.
>
> "Hallowed be thy name, thy kingdom come," the kissing, the pulling and tugging and pushing away.
>
> "Thy will be done, on earth as it is in heaven," clothes disappearing, strange rooms, men who are too strong and too determined.
>
> "Give us this day our daily bread," the sex. Not knowing why I wasn't saying no.
>
> "And forgive us our trespasses," was this me? Was this all my fault? Could I have said no if I wanted to?
>
> "As we forgive those who trespass against us," why do I feel so wronged? Why was he so relieved that I did not say anything? Was I raped?
>
> "And lead us not into temptation, but deliver us from evil," what is wrong with me that I let this happen? How can I sit in church right now when the weight of drunkenness and sex is shrouding me? I know better than this, I am a better person than this. Where did I go?
>
> "For Thine is the kingdom, and the power, and the glory, forever and ever. Amen."

I did not stay for the customary campus ministry dinner after that service. I went to my room because I couldn't stand to look at anyone and did not have the guts to speak out loud. To this day, I still haven't told a soul about what happened.

The common perception of Christians completely ignores the fact that many people who proclaim to be Christian have active and healthy sex lives, sometimes out of wedlock. At some point, being Christian became synonymous with being prudish. This perception contributed to that crippling fear and guilt I felt in the pew. I could not look past the fact that I had had sex to see what about the situation was wrong and unhealthy. I only understood that it happened so I put the blame primarily on myself. I became devastatingly lost between fundamentalist views that perhaps even kissing was a sin out of wedlock, to suddenly finding myself back in a denomination that has not once talked to me about sex. Where were the theological shades of gray when I needed them?

Ultimately, it was my persistent faith that brought me through. I learned to pray and meditate through the crippling cyclical depression I get, learned that God is bigger than just the words on the page and that God cries with the victims at night. God was crying with me on my dark nights, not looking down on me as if I were a harlot to abandon. God was crying with me last night, too, when almost three years later something triggered the memories again. In my faith, I have been able to heal enough to love again, and now have a long-term, wonderful boyfriend. He calls himself a "recovering Catholic," and is spiritual but not religious. It does not matter what he is; he loves me and respects me, unconditionally. We have made the choice to express our love in part by having sex, though that is not something I have talked about or admitted to any of my "church friends."

I am so grateful that I had a campus ministry that accepted me with open arms, without judgments or questions. The transition back into a normal and functional adult life would not have been the same without them, even though they will never know that it was a transition I had to make. At the same time, I wish that our churches were more open to these conversations, to preach, "Don't rape" from the pulpit in a society that teaches girls, "Don't get raped." I wish we preached what is good sex and what is bad sex, what is healthy and what is unhealthy. I wish our churches spoke of sex in a way that removes the shame, and reveals the beauty. *Forever and ever. Amen.*

QUESTIONS FOR DISCUSSION:

1. Potamian addresses how spirituality and faith connected to several of her romantic relationships. What does it look like for faith to support relationships well? When have you seen otherwise?

2. Parties, drinking, and sex feature heavily in Potamian's description of her life immediately after her long-term boyfriend. Are these features of college life unavoidable? What can colleges and universities do to support students like Potamian?

3. The concluding paragraphs call for churches and faith leaders to talk about and claim sex more openly and clearly. How might this look in the contexts you know well?

12

INTERTWINING CYCLES

Michelle Johnson

I crawled into a hot, sticky, sweaty womb. Damp, dark, and pulsing.

On hands and knees I bowed down before entering the *temazcal*, briefly touching my forehead to the ground as a request for permission and to show reverence upon entering the sacred, earthy space.

"Desde lejos, desde lejos oigo," slow, rhythmic words sung, *"el canto enamorado de un pájaro. Ese pájaro es mi abuelo . . . ."* A woman led the chant. I shivered, the rawness of her voice seeping beneath my skin. Soon we all joined in, voices and drums penetrating through thick air. A song of ancestors, of the earth, of birds and creatures and relations we share with one another.

Huddling close, we made room as each person crept inside the small canvas-covered structure. I sat along the edge, as people attending their first time usually do, attempting to lessen the intensity of the heat.

Smoldering rocks arrived, individually marked before being placed in the pit at the center of the circle. As water was poured over them they responded with hissing and steam. My vision blurred, and then, as the canvas door closed: pitch darkness.

"You're okay, you're okay, you're okay." The mantra, trying to convince my heart to stay present. "You'll be okay. Will I be okay? Trust, Michelle."

I sought refuge in my breath. I placed my hands over my belly. Inhale, exhale, inhale. My body gave way to loud outward sighs. I fidgeted, unable to find stillness. I wiggled between my neighbors' sweaty bodies, curling into a fetal position, my right side touching the cool earth. Relief. The ground provided a resting place.

The guides spoke calmly, explaining the ceremony and promising to check on our well-being. Slowly, I surrendered.

We passed through four spiritual doors: of blood relatives, friends, enemies, and ourselves. We prayed and sang. We witnessed each other's struggles and gratitude in the circle. As a group we listened intently to what each person had to share. There were shouts of *¡Aho!*, offerings of acknowledgment and honor given to those present. I felt encouraged to be there fully, without hiding any part of who I was. I felt sadness. Moments resurfaced—ones that I had replayed through my head too many times—of pain, inadequacy, of a looming loneliness. And I felt goodness. Forgiveness. A need to clear out the clutter in my life. The importance of allowing myself to be joyful.

As the ceremony went on I settled into my body. I found a place of groundedness. It came in the form of heightened awareness: salty lips, dripping sweat, *copal* aroma, neighboring bodies and movement. With the small canvas door briefly lifted, I noticed a mother nursing her baby. The baby was cozied up in the mother's arms, calm. I felt protected by this mother, reminded of the beauty of nature, and nurture, and particularly of a woman's body. Sitting in this *temazcal*, the womb of the earth, we found ways to heal and reconnect with the wisdom inside. I thought of my own mother and wombs and the earth. My awareness was shifting.

As a child I was taught to put a piece of straw in the manger every time I did a good deed, my family's goal to prepare a soft, full bed for baby Jesus by Christmas day. In high school I witnessed Catholic social teachings in action while walking alongside *compañeras* and *compañeros* in El Salvador. I boarded a bus with nuns and veterans to travel to Fort Benning, Georgia, in protest of the U.S.-supported militarization of Latin America and other lands. I watched as students at my school were forced to take off rainbow ribbons when the archbishop visited to say mass. And I remember seeing my teacher's face. Torn, she tried to fight back tears.

My Catholic upbringing held moments of aliveness, but I wanted more.

In college I experimented. I went to church and a yearlong Bible study. I spent time in a garden. I met a man who listened. I struggled with my whiteness. I studied my family lineage. I traveled to other countries in the Americas. I tried to regularly prepare nourishing meals. I looked for ways to reconnect with the cultural traditions of my ancestors.

In time I began to discover my church. I began to discover my body.

Eight years after starting to menstruate I touched my menstrual blood for the first time. The consistency was like an egg white: slimy, stretchy, filmy to the touch. A bright, deep color red. As I poured my blood out of the menstrual cup I moved it from one palm to the next, felt it flow back and forth, watching it slide down my fingers and wrists, over curves and hairs, running its course down my wet body. I stood in the shower and studied the bloody mucous cupped in my hand. "This is incredible! This is what comes out of me?"

Growing up I was a master at hiding my tampon. In school I reached in to the deepest pouch in my backpack and then, with my hand still tucked in my bag, slid a tampon up in to my long-sleeved shirt where it would remain until I got past my classmates, past my teacher, past my peers in the girls bathroom. Once I was finally safe in the bathroom stall I removed the tampon that was buried in my shirt sleeve and pushed it up inside of me.

On menstrual days I searched for excuses to tell others why I was tired or not feeling well. I whispered anytime I had to make reference to menstruation and was mortified to think of my dad or brothers seeing a stain on my underwear in the laundry basket at home. So I stayed silent, hiding.

Which is why it was strange, a wonderful sort of strange, to hold my blood in my hands. *Huh.* I had switched to using a menstrual cup because it was better for the environment. It kept disposable pads and tampons out of the landfills. It was less expensive, too. Plus, after having become aware of dioxins and other chemicals in tampons, I didn't feel comfortable putting them in my body. Yet, standing in the shower with blood in my hands I knew this meant something much bigger.

I began to explore my body. Each time I inserted the cup I had to feel around to make sure it was successfully in place. I became interested. What does my body really look like down there? It had been an area from which I was indirectly taught to distance myself. But now, removing the cup I became eager to see the color, consistency, and amount that flowed out of me. I was amazed to think that this thick, filmy flow held many of the nutrients necessary to sustain life. I began to approach my body with awe, curiosity, and respect.

During this same year I was enrolled in a women's studies class. I was struck by how little I knew about the female body and the social issues that surround it. In a PBS film, *The Pill*, we heard stories from Puerto Rican women who in the 1950s and 1960s had been given birth control pills to prevent pregnancy but were never informed that they were part of a clinical trial. The serious side effects experienced by these women, from taking a pill with hormone levels that far exceeded doses allowed today, were largely dismissed. In the documentary *The Business of Being Born*, we explored the topic of childbirth in the United States, questioning how and why certain choices are made. Who are these choices intended to benefit? Considering that birth in the United States is a billion dollar business, how does that influence the wide-ranging options for childbirth such as in homes, at hospitals, in birthing centers, with doctors, midwives, or accompanied by doulas, with varied levels of medical interventions, or none at all? In lectures we raced through topics such as health disparities along class and racial lines, barriers to culturally relevant education and resources, and the complexities of gender and sexuality. I left the class deeply unsettled and fired up to know more.

I learned a lot from outside sources. I also realized, however, that though books and mentors were great, I had the power to become the expert of my own body. I took the initiative to observe. Becoming body literate required paying attention.

I searched for ways to create a relationship with my cycle. I felt that I had been denied something that was mine to explore. I wanted to feel the changes in my body, though they weren't always pleasant. When I was bleeding I stopped taking ibuprofen to numb my discomfort and discovered that a warm bath, a heat pad over my uterus, herbal remedies, time for rest, and sexual intimacy worked better. I noticed the changes in how my body felt depending on stress, and sleep, and the food I put into it. Caffeine and sugar did not make me feel good. Cooked, warm foods did. I discovered that there were times of the month when I was more intuitive, better at making decisions, and more creative. In some cultures menarche was, and in some places still is, a time of celebration and sacred ritual. I craved ritual, so I created a moontime altar. I charted where I was on my cycle, painted images of women and nature, and copied down playwright Ntozake Shange's words "i found god in myself / and i loved her / i loved her fiercely."[1] I felt powerful, assured, moving with a confidence that I hadn't once known.

My legs were spread in the stirrups as I sat waiting for the gynecologist to begin the exam. It was my first OB/GYN appointment. I was twenty-one years old.

"Are you sexually active?" she asked.

"Not now." I said. "My partner and I aren't having sex since we're in the process of learning about the Fertility Awareness Method and other natural options."

The doctor shot me a blank stare, then shook her head.

"I don't recommend that. College students aren't responsible enough to use the Fertility Awareness Method. It's not reliable. Why don't we go ahead and discuss your options with the pill?"

"No. I don't want to put artificial hormones in my body. I have a healthy cycle. I'm not willing to alter that."

"Well, church groups may recommend Natural Family Planning but I don't think it's a good idea. The . . . "

"But, the Fertility Awareness Method and Natural Family Planning aren't the same thing!"

I was dismissed for being a young woman in college. The university health website did not list the Fertility Awareness Method among the options for birth control because it was assumed that I was not capable of knowing my body and using this method responsibly. Yet, I left the office that day feeling like I knew more about natural fertility options than the doctor. I was told that if I wished to be sexually active, medicating and suppressing my body's natural cycle would be the most responsible thing to do.

The first time I tasted food that I had grown was when I worked in a kids' garden. One day, while making salsa with freshly harvested ingre-

---

1. Ntozake Shange, *For Colored Girls Who Have Considered Suicide/When the Rainbow Is Enuf* (New York: Scribner, 1997), 63.

dients, the kids decided to see what raw garlic tasted like. They each popped a clove into their mouths.

"It's spiiiiicy!"

"It burns!"

"Man, you better go get some mint to freshen up yo' breath."

The third-graders were off, sprinting over to the mint patch to stuff their mouths. They raced back with giant grins, teeth laced with flecks of green.

"Hey!" Caleb shouted, "This is like our own version of bubblegum. It's minty fresh garden gum!"

The giggles didn't stop. Another day in the garden.

I fell in love with the land. Not just the land, but what it helped me to be: observant, playful, grounded, gentle. I was nourished. By food, yes, but just as much by the physical movement and the fresh air, by the sound of the birds and the sight of elders tending to their own individual plots. It was a place where I felt community.

After spending a year at the kids' garden I craved more experience with growing food. I found a community-supported agricultural farm and was hired to work as an intern.

I lived on the farm for six weeks during the late-autumn harvest season. The rhythm of my days felt good. Dawn was especially beautiful, laced with morning fog. Outside the farmhouse, I stopped to savor a quiet moment and to watch the wild turkeys make their way across the gravel road. With the sun slowly rising I breathed in the fresh, brisk air of a new day. *Thank you.* Felt prayers became a ritual.

Each day had its challenge, like the day a co-intern and I had to harvest kale in the snow. With fingertips frozen we struggled to make bundles. Thirty-five, thirty-six, thirty-seven . . . would we ever get to one-hundred-and-one bunches? We knew that taking breaks would just make the day longer, but all we wanted was to be inside the warm farmhouse.

In the evenings we relaxed. It felt good that our commute to the "grocery store" meant simply walking out the house door and into the field. We cooked meals together and ate without screens to distract us. We took time to chat, to sit and read, and to can excess produce from the farm. Soon after it was dark I felt ready to climb into bed.

Nighttime was almost completely black. The only light came from the moon and the stars, abundant since we were far from city lights. I slept soundly, tired from the physical work of the day.

During the fall I thought a lot about transformation. My life was in a period of major transition, and I found comfort in witnessing nature moving through its own changes. I harvested from plants that months before were only a fraction of their size. Fast forward a month and the field again looked completely different, covered in a blanket of snow, returned dormant for winter months. The rhythms of life and death were in harmony, each a part of a balancing cycle. And so it was with the soil.

Have you ever tried building a compost pile? This was our major project once the harvest season ended. It was a physically demanding project: uprooting plants, loading them into the truck, and hauling them over to the pile to be dumped. We did this over and over again, pulling out what remained in the field of cabbages, cauliflower, tomatoes, peppers, beans, eggplants—you name it. These plants were combined with buckets of spoiled vegetables, food scraps from cooking in the kitchen, damaged apples, and beer mash from a local brewery. We dreaded having to deal with these buckets. The longer the waste had sat, the worse it smelled. Try dumping out a bucket full of rotten tomatoes that have been rained on and then left to sit out in the sun for weeks. The mold looked like pus and pooled on the top of the bucket. It was a disgusting, necessary part of the job. These were our nitrogen sources.

To make good compost we had to balance the nitrogen material with carbon sources, such as woodchips, sawdust, straw, and cardboard. We created a layered pile, alternating between carbon and nitrogen materials. Providing the right mixture of carbon, nitrogen, water, and oxygen allowed the microorganisms living in the pile to do their work of effectively breaking down the compost. If the pile was not balanced it might have become slimy and smelly, or it might have broken down extremely slowly. With the proper ratios the pile heated up. It took time, yet from it came rich soil that was able to nourish new growth.

At the farm compost pile I imagined what it would look like to build my own pile. I had things to uproot and waste to deal with. There were scraps that reeked from sitting too long: unhealthy self-criticism, family issues, frustration and unresolved tension with former housemates.

Physical labor became a method of opening up channels to release stagnant energy in my body.

As I began to build my compost pile there was a part of me that was angry. I had let food go to waste. There were opportunities I had wanted to accept but hadn't taken, moments I didn't enjoy because I let someone else's opinion hold me back, ways in which I had made a habit out of putting myself down. For a long time I had held on to this rotten food. I didn't know what to do with it. By building the compost pile on the farm I began to consider how I could transform waste into something useful. What was I willing to work for? I uprooted what did not serve me, carried its weight over to the pile, and dumped it.

Emerging from my compost were seeds that began to sprout. So much comes down to the health of the soil.

While studying abroad in Chile I attended a four-day gathering in which indigenous elders shared in ceremony and teachings. In one workshop an elder spoke to a group of fifty of us, congregated together under the shade of a large tree. We sat shoulder to shoulder, a whole herd of sisters and brothers. I was consumed by the presence of this woman. It was one of goodness, radiant joy, an inner peacefulness and strength.

"I am an elder of the moon lodge," she said. "My job is to create a calm and nourishing place for the women of my community during their moontime, during their sacred time of bleeding."

"When women live in close relation with one another, their cycles sync and they bleed at the same time. This is nature's way of designing us to be in communion with one another. We honor this time for a woman. The village takes over her tasks so that she, and the other women on their moontimes, can go to the moon lodge to rest and release their energy."

My eyes brightened. She continued,

There is a pit in the center of the tipi over which the women can squat as a way to physically bleed onto the earth. We all sleep around this pit, with our heads close to the center. You see, a woman's most powerful time is when she's bleeding. It is a time to pay attention to one's dreams in order to receive knowledge and wisdom. Our revelations benefit our communities.

The stories shared by the elder echoed themes I hoped for in my life: a respect for my bleeding time as a time to slow down, a ritual coming together of women, a community's support, and the valuing of listening to our bodies' needs.

I started making my moontime a time of rest. I noticed how tired my body was during this time, and how much my thoughts became inwardly focused. I practiced saying no to events and tasks. And I came to understand the importance of support from a whole community.

I shared what I was experiencing with my partner. He encouraged me. One day he called to say that he found the book *Taking Charge of Your Fertility* by Toni Weschler, at the thrift store. He had known how much I wanted it to use as a resource. He read it cover to cover, amazed at how much he had learned, and wanting to work together to chart my cycle. When I was on my moontime he knew if I wasn't feeling well and offered to make me a meal, rub my back, or just let me be. I appreciated his support.

Setting time aside was not always easy. I was a full-time student, I volunteered, and I actively participated in two organizations. I tried to work with whatever time I had. Some days a half hour of quiet was all I could find, but that time proved to be significant. The feeling of being rejuvenated stuck with me, setting the tone for the next month.

I use the word *moontime* to refer to menstruation, to articulate the way human cycles are intertwined with those of nature. My cycle is connected to the moon and to the seasons. Everything I was doing in the garden, on hands and knees dirty with soil, and while in the *temazcal*, also had everything to do with reconnecting with my body. As I began to touch, observe, respect, and enter into relation with earth and body I experienced love and gratitude for both.

I've found faith in bleeding, planting seeds, and noticing cycles intertwining. In appreciating my body and listening to what it needs. I've found faith through movement and my sexuality and in expression. In healthy relationships. I've found faith in witnessing the untamed nature of a baby. In peers who are engaging in living simply. In elders reminding me of traditions worth reclaiming: like preparing sauerkraut, reusing items repeatedly, working with our hands, visiting the neighbors, and being outdoors.

I never expected to experience the sacred in a college bathroom, nor in a pile of rotting mush. Yet the divine was there. I've learned to pay attention.

When I exited the *temazcal* I felt nauseous. I tried to stand. I wanted to join the others in the circle in bringing the ceremony to a close, but I felt incredibly weak. I laid my body back down on the ground, closed my eyes, and rested. Soon the circle dispersed and everyone began to share food and drinks.

"*¿Cómo te sientes?*" my friend asked.

"*Mareada, con ganas de vomitar.*" "Dizzy," I told him, "wanting to throw up."

We sat. I focused on breathing. I was given sections of an orange to eat. Then my friend placed his hand on my shoulder. He said that sometimes when someone exits feeling dizzy it can be a sign of imbalance in that person's life. With tears forming I leaned my body into his, his arms wrapping me tight.

Being inside the *temazcal* reconnected me with roots. I was rebound with nature. The ceremonial gestation provided me with nourishment and time to grow. I crawled out red, wet, and crying. Overwhelmed. Reborn. I was given food and had earth and family to hold me.

It was true that I had been feeling very off-balance, so scattered in my life. I had become distracted. Exiting the *temazcal* I was brought back to the basics. I needed nature and nurture. I needed food, water, touch, and shelter. I needed love and connection.

When I unraveled my heap of clothes to change after the ceremony a white feather appeared. It was small enough to fit in to my outstretched hand. I wrapped each finger, one by one, gently around the feather, wanting to memorize how it felt. It was soft and fluffy at the bottom, smooth and flat in the center and top. It had a thick center shaft that held it together.

Birds are messengers of the Creator. They help to bring connection and communication between the Creator and creation. Feathers are blessings, prayers, messages. The meaning of a feather most depends on the bird that it comes from, but the color can also be important. White represents sacred light and purity; white animals are often rare in their species so their energy is special. I accepted this feather as a gift from this bird and from the Creator, encouraging me to continue on this path, reassuring me that this is how I would regain balance. I lifted this feather up to my heart, at peace.

Be good to yourself, Michelle. Honor nature and all those you meet. Notice the cycles. They all intertwine.

QUESTIONS FOR DISCUSSION:

1. Much of North American culture, and perhaps especially Christian culture, eschews deep connections with physical, embodied identity. What educational experiences—from organic farms to college classrooms—can aid in a conversation to reclaim bodies as sacred? Alternatively, is it somehow unwise to broach such discussions at colleges and universities?

2. Johnson clearly has a gift for thoughtful reflection, for deep reconsideration of cultural assumptions and values. In doing so, Johnson attempts to make new connections to her body, to her food, to her faith, and to her neighbors. How can we aid young adults in making such connections? What stops us from doing so?

13

OUT OF THE CLOSET AND BACK TO CHURCH

Kyle J. Thorson

My early faith journey was fairly representative of small town North Dakota. I was read Bible stories as a child, attended regular worship and Sunday school at the church that both confirmed me and gave me my first Communion, saw a controversy within the church with a (gasp) "woman pastor" who was deemed too radical, participated in a small prayer group at school, and taught a fifth grade Sunday school class. In short, I took my faith seriously and generally accepted the rules, guidelines, and laws that the church trumpeted as necessary for following Jesus.

My thoughts and instincts growing up were conservative. I remember a discussion with some of my classmates in which I firmly stated that after I was married, if my wife died, I would never remarry because the Bible states you could only marry one person. I also knew that homosexuality was a sin and that African tribes who hadn't heard about Jesus would still be saved because they didn't know any better. I figured the same rule applied to unbaptized babies. John 3:16 had been ingrained into my psyche throughout Sunday school—well, one interpretation of it, at least.

By the time I enrolled at the University of North Dakota, I was filled with supposed solutions to a variety of the world's problems. Perhaps like most eighteen-year-olds, I thought I knew everything. Imagine my dismay, then, when what I found at UND was not more answers, but more questions. Instead of memorizing the Ten Commandments, I found myself having to think critically about the world around me. I suddenly had to justify my beliefs and answers; I couldn't just say things were true without thoughtful support.

I soon struggled with doubt and disbelief. I couldn't figure out how to protect my house of cards from falling as the questions around me threatened. I did what seemed most logical at the time: I stopped engaging the questions. It appeared to me that the more questions I asked myself about my beliefs, the more I couldn't fit God into my old box of faith. I began to hate all religion since it was full of incomplete answers that didn't connect to the real world. So my solution for the first two years of college: avoid religion altogether.

Yet, even as I abandoned religion, I wasn't willing to give up my sense of spirituality. I still found relationships holy, which drove my desire to help others in the world. Despite my struggles with faith, I felt that I couldn't give up on God. After all, I still believed in and loved God; the contradictions and unanswered questions were what I wanted to turn from. I immediately began to identify as "spiritual but not religious." By doing so, I could avoid church and religion, but still be in a relationship with God.

And then came the Holy Spirit.

A few of my good friends were part of a deacon group at Christus Rex, UND's Lutheran Campus Ministry. At some point in time, they convinced me to come to a worship service with them. I was a little apprehensive, but I decided since I had attended worship only a handful of times in the last year (read: over Christmas and Easter break I played trumpet for my home congregation) that I would go with them. Plus, I was told that the first worship of the school year came with a free prime rib dinner. I practically leapt out of bed on Sunday morning and went to church. What college student doesn't love free food?

I can still see the pictures in my head from that first day. I was almost overwhelmed. A very loud woman named Jo immediately greeted me. "HELLO! My name is Jo. Do you sing?" Jo was always recruiting for the choir. Upon sheepishly denying her request to join the choir, she introduced me to a number of people, including Kathy Fick, the campus minister. I think I met about fifteen new people that day.

When it was time to go, Kathy caught me at the door. She thanked me for coming and asked why I hadn't come more frequently with

Ryan, who was part of the deacon group. I stumbled over my words trying to think of a good reason to give her. Before I answered, she had already decided that I would certainly like to help with one of the upcoming events and that Ryan would bring me along. Before I knew it I had agreed. It took about two months before I was invited to join the deacon program. It seemed the Holy Spirit knew what I needed even before I did.

Around this time, I became depressed. I stopped going out with my friends so I could sit at home by myself. When I was with friends, I couldn't focus or have fun. I became uncontrollably sad. At the time I thought I was hiding my true feelings quite well. I prided myself on listening to other people's problems and never revealing any of my own. But, in hindsight, it's clear my friends were wiser than I knew. They could tell I was depressed. My wake-up call was coming.

One week before my twenty-first birthday, my friends made a plan. Mind you, this was a terrible plan, but somehow it worked out well. They decided that I, who had never been drunk in his life, would take shots of alcohol until I was ready to fess up to what was going on in my life. I'm still not sure who thought of this plan, but once it was created my friends leapt into action.

I remember the first shot. I was so scared to take it. How would it make me feel? Would it taste good? Would I get caught? Would I die from an overdose? I stared at the shot glass with clear liquid and gave everyone reasons why I shouldn't drink it. But with peer pressure at its best, my seven friends made me take the first shot of my life. It burned and it tasted gross. After a while, my lips started tingling. I had another.

Looking back, I'm not sure why I decided to go along with the drinking. Perhaps somewhere deep inside, a part of me wanted to do it. I wanted to drown my feelings and feel something else—happiness even. I wanted to let go and have fun. I wanted to feel connected with my friends and the world after feeling so lonely. Within an hour, I was locked in the bedroom crying with two of my best friends who desperately tried to get me to tell them what was wrong. I couldn't hold it in any longer.

"I'm gay!"

As I spat the words from my mouth, I felt an immediate sense of relief. As many young gay men, I was deeply afraid of my peers' reaction once I outted myself. But, their reaction didn't substantiate that fear. They hugged me and cried. "Oh, we thought you were dying or something!" They both confirmed to my drunken self that it was going to be OK. They assured me that I was still going to be their friend and that they still indeed did love me. And just like that, after feeling so alone in my sadness, I had friends to share my journey. I began to tell them everything.

My coming out posed a key problem: Throughout my life, I had truly believed that I would grow up, get married, have children, live a long and happy life, and eventually die of old age. Everything that I was taught growing up seemed to point to homosexuality as *unnatural* and *immoral*. I was confident that in my entire hometown of 3,500 people, nobody had ever been gay. Furthermore, my church was pretty clear: gay people led lives of *sin* and were to spend eternity in hell.

I didn't fully understand I was gay until the summer before my twenty-first birthday. Well, I knew that I was attracted to men, but I never thought it was possible to have a relationship with them. I had bought into the theology that God wanted traditional marriage and normal families—after all, it was all I knew. I simply couldn't imagine how gay couples worked. It wasn't an option for me. And then, one day, I fell for a stupid boy. That stupid boy opened my eyes. He was also why I had been horribly depressed. And until I came out to my friends, there was no one I could talk to about him, my sexuality, or my faith.

Coming out freed me to engage tough questions. How could I be gay? I really did love God, but how could I love him and be attracted to men at the same time? Did God find that, find me, *abominable*? What if my family found out and never spoke to me again? While I had a few friends who would support me, I still wondered if other friends would abandon me. Would the world still see me as a good person?

Enter Kathy, my pastor at Christus Rex. I remember being invited into her office and sitting on her green couch to talk about life. As I sat there, I nervously stuttered, "I don't know, I'm fine." "Really, Kyle? Fine?" she replied. I knew what I wanted to say, but couldn't get it out. It was just as hard to say it the second time as it was the first. I'm surprised she didn't leave me sitting alone on the couch with all the question avoiding I was doing. Finally, I came around. "I'm gay." Relief rushed over me.

Her reply surprised me: "God still loves you and anyone who says differently has flawed theology." Wait. What? You mean that God was big enough to love even me? I began to see a glimpse of the faith that I currently hold, one that indeed has room enough for everyone without exception.

Soon after meeting with Kathy, my faith began to flourish again. Hungry for the study and conversation that Christus Rex provided, I ended my two-year faith famine with a voracious appetite. Every Wednesday at deacons, I found myself relishing the very questions that I had once feared. I listened to the older deacons and challenged myself to push at the sides of my boxes. I went to every Bible study, worship service, and social event that I could. I fell in love with God anew and I started to find a family at Christus Rex. It became my home away from home.

Campus ministry became the defining factor for my college faith journey. While at the University of North Dakota, I developed a better sense of how big the world really is and how we're called to serve God in it. My university classes were designed to spur students to think critically about real world situations and ask better questions. These skills began to shape my faith as well. I became aware of biblical themes and contemplated their complex meaning.

I participated in interfaith experiences on campus that helped me make connections between Judaism, Christianity, and Islam. The freedom to explore other faiths also helped me identify my own beliefs. It enabled me to build relationships with a wide variety of people and consider the possibility of my call within the framework of the larger church.

By my senior year, I began to explore the possibility of a year of service through the Young Adults in Global Mission (YAGM) program of the Evangelical Lutheran Church in America (ELCA). I began the application essays to further reflect on whether or not YAGM would be a good fit for me. As I continued the application process, it became clear that submitting my application felt right, and I was eventually invited to interview for, and ultimately participate in, the program.

Since the YAGM program and the ELCA were fully accepting of me as a gay man, they worked to find a country placement that had strong in-service support structure and a culture in which I wouldn't have to hide my sexuality. Luckily, there was a place for me at YAGM's site in Mexico. It quickly found a place in my heart, and my year of service helped me think even more deeply about the needs of the church and the world.

My denomination often asks how we might better welcome young adults. It's a complex question with many responses, but my experience may be illustrative. My withdrawal from the church was partly a result of my longing to be a part of a church that had room for my whole self. I couldn't be involved if I constantly felt shamed by my questions and my identity. Eventually, I understood that welcome, and came to recognize God's love was big enough for me. God can handle my tensions, and questions, and doubts. Many people welcomed me back into the church, regardless of my sexual orientation. With God's help, I felt whole again—even healed.

College transformed me from a shy conservative closeted boy with all the answers to an openly-gay man willing to engage in questions of faith, and feel like part of God's church. My time at UND and Christus Rex showed me a faith that is inviting, wonderful, and too beautiful not to be true.

QUESTIONS FOR DISCUSSION:

1. For Thorson, claiming the label "spiritual but not religious" seems to have been an important step whereby he could acknowledge God, but step back from institutional religion. Why are the ranks of *spiritual but not religious* college students growing?

2. The process of engaging new questions critically was essential to Thorson's college experience. How can colleges support students emotionally as their classes push critical study that may upset previously held assumptions?

3. The invitation, welcome, and continued support of a campus ministry helped Thorson immensely. What positive ministry practices might be gleaned from Thorson's story?

Section IV

Walking with Others
(Or, Sometimes, Running from Them)

Learning is a collaborative process; so too is faithful living. At times, however, a college campus filled with thousands of students can feel as lonely as a prison cell. A colleague of mine sometimes gives students a difficult assignment: Find a quiet spot outside or a room by yourself, turn off all your digital devices and just be. By yourself. For an hour. The students' response ranges from outrage to bliss.

When I return to the college I attended for a visit, I usually try to find a few moments to myself. I'll use these to go on a walk in the woods and find the spot where I sat for twenty minutes each week one semester, required reflection for a class journaling assignment on nature and solitude. I'll also visit "my spot" on the fifth floor of the library where I read hundreds of pages (and took the occasional nap before getting kicked out when the library closed at 2 a.m.). But these reminiscent times of solitude only come after I visit my old professors, send a group text message to my college friends, and share a picture of campus on Facebook. My visits back to campus reflect a complicated balance of community and solitude.

Essays in Section IV consider the back-and-forth journey of individual self-discovery and support from others. The stories are diverse. Pivotal settings include a homestay balcony in Spain and a frat house in Tennessee. Allison Chubb in "Blossoms in the Desert" writes of her college experience "physicalizing," and her sometimes-problematic experience of support. "Finding God on Frat Row" by Michael Casey W. Woolf defies many stereotypes of faith and fraternities (and leaves a few intact). In "Three Parties," Lauren Deidra Sawyer writes of the excitement of illicit alcohol and the community it supports. Finally, Br. Lawrence A. Whitney's essay, "Faith Transforms in Times of Crisis" covers the remarkable journey of his faith experience on college campuses from student to pastor, mourner to minister. Each of the stories is personal; so too are they communal.

14

BLOSSOMS IN THE DESERT

Allison Chubb

It was at a small party in our friends' basement suite that I handed a tiny razor blade to my friend Heather, instructing her never to return it. She looked confused.

"What is this?" she asked, misunderstanding my cryptic behavior. "I don't know why you're giving me this."

Disappointed but a bit relieved, I realized she had no idea that I'd started cutting only a few weeks before. Part of me wished I could tell her everything, but the voice of reason said it was better not to draw that kind of attention to myself. Even from Heather.

I'd played with self harm off and on in high school, but what I was experiencing now was getting out of my control. I was scared. "The thing is," I told myself, "I'm not crazy; I'm just unduly realistic." Life was a dark and difficult place and I was one of the few willing to admit to it. I hated myself for my perceived inability to make any real difference in the world.

Seven months previously, I began my BA in TESOL (Teachers of English to Speakers of Other Languages) at a Christian college, hoping that I could, "enable people to pull themselves out of poverty," as I put it. At starry-eyed eighteen, I had every intention of crossing the globe and ultimately changing the world.

Yet as my freshman year wore on, time after time I found myself lying on the floor of my dorm room, crying out to God for the needs of the world. I had been aware of pain and suffering before, but studying anthropology, theology, and sociology was only serving to broaden my awareness of the immense gap between the longings of the world and the kingdom for which we prayed. The majority of my classmates, I concluded rather self-righteously, were blissfully unaware of how privileged we were in comparison with the world's majority.

Expressing the turmoil I faced on the inside by some kind of outward action wasn't new for me. I am a hopelessly kinesthetic learner and constantly mirror my inner life in my body language. "Yes, Allison? You have a question," my linguistics professor informed me during class one morning. I hadn't put my hand up.

"What?" I smiled, impressed that she could read my mind.

"Your face is all scrunched up, the way it is when you have a question," Professor Rust laughed.

On several occasions, I showed up at school wearing black, my head covered as I spent the day in prayer for the Church. Neither my professors nor my classmates generally noticed, but dressing differently was a way of expressing the myriad of questions rushing through my mind about who I was and what God was up to in the world. "You're a physicalizer," my professors used to tell me.

The following October, my "physicalizing" got out of hand. Sitting in a theater classroom with the other students who were cast for the upcoming production, we went through the script for the first time, a story about a young woman who dies "a terrible death" by drinking disinfectant. Returning to my dorm room after the reading, I was overwhelmed by my identification with the nameless young woman. She was right; life really was uncertain and painful and lonely. There was no use in fighting the darkness like this.

Kneeling on the floor as the wind howled outside, a sense of intense loneliness and fear overwhelmed me.

"Where are you, God? I can't do this anymore. It's too much, . . . and *who* are you, really? Are you there or is this all just a joke? Why is fighting to live so hard? The only thing I hope for is to be of use to you in the world, . . . but I'm afraid that will never happen. The needs of the world are too great, and I am too small. I'm so alone."

I wandered into the bathroom and found some disinfectant, just to look at it. Drinking only a *little* of this particular disinfectant shouldn't do damage, so I figured I might as well try it. Life felt pretty pointless anyway. And I couldn't stop thinking about the poor young woman who died a terrible death. I reached for the white lid and poured some into it, paying careful attention to how much I drank. The bathroom swirled around me until all I could see was the little cup in my hand. As if controlled by something outside myself, I was startled as the liquid burned its way down my throat. I shouldn't have been surprised; it was exactly the way it would have felt if I was dressing an open wound.

In a moment of clarity, I realized that I needed to tell someone what I was doing before continuing to drink from the bottle sitting in front of me. Without thinking, I jumped up and forced myself out the back door and across the yard, my head pulsing wildly. What I needed was someone who would hold me accountable, someone who wouldn't be shocked but would understand the importance of walking me through this. Now was not the time for a Christian lecture. Now was not the time to be misunderstood.

Fall leaves crunched under my feet and the sun was beginning to set as I found myself heading toward Rachel's room, a classmate who struggled with bulimia. Rachel would understand without lecturing me or turning me in to the residence director because she knew what it was like to hurt as I did and to feel misunderstood. As I struggled to sort out my racing thoughts, I had a distinct sense of the Holy One walking with me across the lawn that day. In the midst of the pain and confusion cluttering my mind, it was almost as if Jesus himself were leading me away from harm. It felt like we were alone together in the world.

Reaching Rachel's room a few minutes later, I was relieved to find that she was available, welcoming me in her arms like Christ. I had isolated myself so completely that I'd forgotten what it was like to be cared for by a friend. Rachel felt like a refuge as I poured out my story, not knowing where to begin or end. "I only came here," I finished, "because I knew it would help me not to drink any more of the disinfectant."

Rachel listened quietly, giving me her full attention. She did not act like I was crazy and she did not overreact and run for help. She did exactly what I had hoped she would: embody Jesus for me so I could bring my racing mind back to this time and place. "It's okay, Allison," she comforted me, "I know what it's like to hate yourself. This will pass and it will get better." I knew she was right. Hearing her say those words was enough for me to wrestle free from the young woman's story in the play. The darkness would not stretch on forever.

As we continued to talk, I saw Rachel's residence assistant out of the corner of my eye, talking on the phone in the hallway. Could she hear us, I wondered? But I didn't care. Things were going to be okay, and that was all that mattered. I hadn't swallowed enough disinfectant to do any damage; I knew that for sure. These things were always well calculated.

I was surprised, then, when just a few minutes later our residence director walked into Rachel's room, a look of purpose and concern across her face. "What happened, Allison?" she asked me intently.

"Um . . . it's fine," I assured her, a little annoyed by the intensity of her presence. "I didn't drink very much." I saw the residence assistant standing in the hallway.

"How do you know?" the director persisted. "I think we should take you to the hospital."

By now I was feeling rather embarrassed. "No, really" I begged, "I don't need to go. I didn't drink enough. It's not that poisonous!" This was exactly what I was hoping to avoid: being misunderstood and not listened to. I'd been to the hospital before and I had no intention of going again. That's why I forced myself not to drink any more. Why wasn't the director listening to me?

The woman standing in front of me interrupted my thoughts. "I'm sorry, but you need to go. Come on." I could tell there was no arguing my way out of this, so I slowly slid off Rachel's bed and followed our residence director out of the room. I glanced back at Rachel over my shoulder, wondering if she understood.

Is that why we never expose our eating disorders and self-injury? I wondered. Because we know that people won't know what to do with us? But it was too late for those kinds of questions. Suddenly my condition was being treated more seriously than it needed to be, and I began to feel sorry for myself. Perhaps I was in real danger. Maybe I was going to die.

On the way to the hospital, Jesus sat beside me holding my hand. I felt sick and overwhelmed, but not because of the disinfectant. I continued to wonder who I was and what on earth God was up to in my life. My head was spinning. Lights sped by on either side of the vehicle. It was dark.

Twenty minutes later, my three escorts and I found ourselves registering at the emergency desk assisted by one of my professor's wives.

The world is embarrassingly small sometimes, I thought to myself. I was reluctant to release any personal information, feeling quite unsure of who I really was. I had hoped to reinvent myself during college, but so far it was not going well.

Fortunately we didn't have a long wait before I was taken to be examined, two college staff members and my own residence assistant along for the ride. I was frustrated and confused as the doctor insisted on sticking a huge needle into my wrist despite my protests that I hadn't drunk enough disinfectant to cause any damage. While he struggled to find a vein in my wrist, it felt as if he was attempting to cut my hand right off. Never had I experienced this kind of pain. Was it exacerbated by the emotional nature of the situation? I couldn't tell. This was certainly unlike any needle I had received before. I had no idea how much time was going by, but it felt like hours. And, as I had predicted, no damage had been done.

After being taken to the hospital that night, I became increasingly wary of with whom I talked about my internal struggles and fears. Yet as misunderstood as I had felt, the sense of Jesus sitting beside me holding my hand never went away. God became my ever-present refuge, the one who walked beside me and carried my fears when they were too much for me to bear.

Faithful was the word I used to describe God in those days. God was the friend, the mother, the teacher I needed so desperately. I was comforted by the belief that when I could not understand my own confusion, God knew exactly what was happening and was in control even when I was not. And the people who most exemplified this showed me what God was like.

My friend Nan was one such person. Nan was twelve years older than I and we'd known one another off and on since I was a toddler. I could tell Nan anything at all and be sure that she wouldn't be shocked or, even worse, jump to conclusions. Through her tender guidance I had some success with putting an end to my self-injury, not because she told me it was wrong or harmful, but because she was gentle with me. Nan was the person I went to when I needed to experience "Jesus with skin on" because she did not pretend there were easy answers to the things I was experiencing. She seemed to intuit that matters of life and faith are never black-and-white, a refreshing change from the regimented religion of my childhood.

I spent my third year of college completing my internship and abstaining from self-injury entirely, but during the winter of my final year I began cutting again. I was living alone and God seemed particularly far away. "Physicalizing" my confusion came naturally for me, the way it always had. As graduation loomed closer, I wondered where I would go and what I would do after I finished. This small college community had become home for me and I dreaded having to start all over again.

I knew that cutting was ultimately not the best way to deal with my pain and confusion, but I also couldn't come up with a good enough reason to stop. Sure, our bodies are temples of the Holy Spirit, I would tell myself, but this is more complicated than that. I needed some way of expressing the darkness within me, and this seemed to be supporting my efforts to live a normal life apart from my deafening silence. Surely if God wanted me to have a better coping mechanism, God would provide that for me. Surely God understood the darkness that clouded my mind during those times alone in my apartment.

And sure enough, God was particularly close to me during those times of darkness, much like the time that Jesus held my hand on the way to the hospital that warm fall evening two years before. My faith had changed significantly over the last three-and-a-half years, growing deep roots that nourished my soul during times of drought like this. Throughout those years I had experienced things that left me feeling betrayed by friends, family, the mental health system, and even the Church, but never by God. It was prayer, particularly embodied, "physicalized" prayer, that sustained me through those days when I felt like I had no one left in the world.

I found this kind of life with God in the most varied of places: kneeling with a candle in a basement of the college, burning a list of my sins in the woods at night, talking to a huge statue of the Virgin Mary, and learning to walk a labyrinth. I learned that when we act out our prayers the way we do while walking a labyrinth, we stimulate our right brain, the creative center that longs to encounter God with all the joy and abandon of a child. When I prayed with my right brain, the studied logic of my left brain had to be quieted for a while as I sat in wonder at the feet of Jesus.

And time and time again, God would remind me that I was mistaken—I was *not* alone. People like Rachel or Nan would come into my life just when I felt like I could no longer bear the darkness alone. Through them I learned what it means to be the hands and feet of Jesus in the world: not necessarily to traverse the globe and eradicate poverty (an impossible task for one young woman!) but to embody the quiet tenderness of the Holy One to my classmates, professors, and friends. To my neighbors.

"Kara," I confided in my favorite professor one afternoon in my final year of college, "Can you give me a reason to stop cutting? I keep trying to come up with one but I can't." I must have pushed the poor woman to her limit of compassion some days; I was forever dropping into her office to unload the questions that burdened me. This latest quandary was entirely outside of her job description.

I watched the woman in her early thirties intently, glancing down at her bright red heels to hide my embarrassment. Her dark brown curls framed her face, matching her black-rimmed glasses and making her the most beautiful academic I had ever seen. "Well," she began thoughtfully, "Does cutting bring you closer to God?"

Curses! I thought to myself. Kara was always turning my questions back on me like that. In hindsight, I realize that she was teaching me to rely on God instead of on her. She might not be around the next time I entered a spiritual wilderness, but God certainly would be.

"Actually . . . it does," I answered cautiously, knowing that wasn't the answer she was looking for. "I've never felt as close to God as I do when I'm cutting." I thought of my worst and most recent episode that nearly landed me in the hospital for the third time. Jesus had been almost tangibly present.

"Oh really?" she asked with genuine curiosity. "Well, . . . all of our lives are intended to honor God, right? How does this honor God?" The question didn't have a hint of judgment. She had no idea that her words had just marked a turning point in my life.

"It doesn't," I agreed simply. "You're right, it doesn't. I want everything I do to give God glory, . . . and this is something that doesn't do that. Which is reason enough to stop doing it."

"You know, maybe that's a better way to think about it then," she mused out loud, unsure of what else to say.

But she didn't need to say anything else. I knew that God was beginning to bring me out the other side of this desert. Leaving her office, I thought of Frank Laubach, a missionary who had committed to living every minute of every day with his attention fixed on God. "What, [O

God], do you desire said?" he wrote. "What, Father, do you desire done this minute?"[1]

As I struggled to stop cutting over the next couple of months, it felt like wrestling a demon. The darkness would return just when I thought I had mastered it, and I was driven to my knees time and again. I lamented the loss of innocence in my faith; I no longer found God in the moments of "spiritual high" the way I did at the beginning of college. Now God was found in the stillness, the space created within me by sitting in a silent church surrounded by flickering candles and icons. Above all, I could no longer pretend that life was not hard; it was. My hope lay in the knowledge that God walks along beside us, teaching us to learn from the one whose yoke is easy and whose burden is light.

When I entered college my faith was essentially an intellectual one. I experienced God by believing certain things and acting in very particular ways. Four years later, the wilderness I had experienced there transformed my faith into one which was much more embodied, settled deeply into the darkest corners of my being. I learned to pray the Jesus Prayer when I could utter no words of my own, to light a candle when I felt surrounded by darkness, to dance alone in my room when the darkness lifted.

The Jesus Prayer was a faithful companion particularly when I was afraid or anxious and needed to be brought back to the present moment. Sitting nervously in my therapist's waiting room, I would use it to root me in the great healer, fingering each knot in my Eastern Orthodox prayer rope: "Lord Jesus Christ, Son of God, have mercy on me a sinner. Lord Jesus Christ, Son of God, have mercy on me a sinner. Lord Jesus Christ, Son of God, have mercy on me a sinner."

In time, embodying my pain by cutting turned into embodying my faith through ancient ritual. I found that when I was carrying too much, I could symbolically leave my load in the center of a labyrinth. When I was restless, I began to carry prayer beads that kept my hands and mind focused on God. I have now come to see the passionate "physicalizing" that caused me so much pain in college as a gift that enables me to see the hand of God in each leaf, each child, each breath of wind.

---

1. Frank Charles Laubach, "Frank Laubach's Letters by a Modern Mystic," *Christian Spirituality*, ed. Frank Magill and Ian McGreal (San Francisco: Harper and Row, 1988), 516–520, accessed July 24, 2014, http://www.dwillard.org/articles/artview.asp?artID=43.

Six years after I stopped cutting, I catch a glimpse of faded scars as I raise my arms before a waiting congregation, holding out for them, "the blood of Christ, shed for you." They are invited forward to take part in the greatest ritual of healing the world has ever known: the Eucharist, the Great Thanksgiving, when we are invited into the death and resurrection of Christ. Lifting the wine to a teenager's lips as tears well up in his eyes, I am keenly reminded of God's faithfulness through my own desert and the people God placed there to journey with me. I now journey with this young man as his college chaplain, learning to trust the quiet handiwork of God in the life of another.

I do not know why some people are freed from the darkness and others remain there for a lifetime, but God is surely able to make blossoms bloom in any desert. Every day on campus I see myself in the eyes of my students and I am awed again by the new life God can breathe into the soul of a deeply confused young woman. As we pray together at the closing of the Eucharist each week, God can surely do, "More than we can ask or imagine (Eph. 3:20). Thanks be to God!"

QUESTIONS FOR DISCUSSION

1. When the residence director insisted Chubb be taken to the hospital, she asks herself, "Is that why we never expose our eating disorders and self-injury? Because we know that people won't know what to do with us?" How would you answer her? What would you say to the residence director?
2. Share some of your own experiences with physicalizing, or embodied, faith practices. How can, or should, we use such practices with college students?
3. Chubb's professors, especially Kara, play an important role in her story. What professors have been instrumental in your life? How would you have responded if you were in Kara's position?

15

FINDING GOD ON FRAT ROW

Michael Casey W. Woolf

Extreme nerves—that's how I'd describe it. On the day I was going to be initiated into the Chi Phi fraternity, my heart was beating so fast it was ready to leap out of my chest. I can still recall the ceaseless repetition, prayerlike, as I muttered the fraternity's long and storied history to myself. The fraternity's twelve founders, its triple-origin, eventual merger, and maxims blended together as I lost track of time. Had I been waiting for hours, minutes, or days? The suit and tie I wore at the time clung to my body and made me painfully aware of how much I was sweating. But the thing I remember most clearly is the pride that I felt when someone called me "brother" for the first time. It was and still is quite simply the best moment of my short life. I went into a hidden room as a candidate and emerged as full-fledged member of the oldest college Greek-letter fraternity in existence. One does not do that everyday.

In November of 2008 I was initiated into the Chi Phi fraternity at the University of Tennessee—Knoxville. I knew little then about the surprising ways my fraternity would shape me over the course of my college experience. While I joined Chi Phi in an attempt to become involved on campus and have fun doing it, my chapter offered far more than that. At its core, my fraternity gave me a lens with which to see the world, and just as surely as it changed how I viewed friendship or molded my leadership ability, it also altered my relationship to my faith, to God, and to my fellow human beings.

When I came to the University of Tennessee, there was little expectation that I would join a fraternity, let alone eventually become the chapter's president. I entered my freshman year with a sense that I was called to ministry. But I wondered if fraternity life would be compatible with becoming a minister. After all, no ministers I knew had told me college stories about fraternity parties or pledging. As it turns out, Chi Phi was not just any fraternity. In fact, when I arrived on campus it was not even a functional fraternity at all, but an interest group seeking to resurrect a chapter recently gone dormant.

After talking to a few members of the interest group and national staff, I became intrigued with the idea of starting *something new*. And so we did. We recruited new members, learned the history and ritual of our fraternity, had philanthropy events, held weekly meetings, mixers and formals, and, of course, parties. But we also did something more than that: we formed a community. We lived together, we ate together, and, perhaps most importantly, we were present for one another. It was this simple act of being together—of creating something that had not been there before—that radically transformed both my understanding of *call*, and my view of God.

Raised as a conservative Southern Baptist, I learned a very particular type of Christian narrative growing up. In the stories of my childhood, an interesting thing happened—the individual became the center of the Christian universe. Faith was about personal salvation, personal witness, inviting God into *your* heart, *you* must come and be baptized, Jesus died for *you singular*. Now that I had become brothers with these people, that all seemed very strange. Where were all the other people in the pews? What were they doing? Were we all just sitting in a room together having individual experiences and sometimes, but not very often, telling each other about them? While my brothers remained in bed sleeping off their latest hangover, I went to church, and I carried memories of last night's party with me into that place.

What challenged me was that I seemed to be having my most spiritually connected experiences with *other people* in community, and not at church. And, of course, though I felt guilty about it, I'm not alone. Many young adults have experienced the same feeling of spiritual connection outside of church, but lack of connection inside a congregation.

This disconnect causes many to avoid darkening the doors of churches for years; they already have what they want.

I remember how dull church seemed the morning after sharing a cigar with my brother on the sort of cool autumn evening that all true Tennesseans know. As we smoked our (probably fake) Cuban cigars that he had bought in the Bahamas, we talked about God, the holy, and salvation. If you were there that night, listening only literally, you would have mostly heard us discussing the kind of lives we imagined for ourselves, what we wanted to do when we "grew up," and of course, the Halloween party next weekend. Monster Mash was, after all, the biggest party of the year.

For me, however, the conversation was spiritual in a way that rivaled the great stories I had grown up with. Here was Mary's annunciation, the burning bush, and Gideon's angel all in one. What more could you ask for? Everything superfluous seemed to disappear, and before I knew it, four hours had passed and our voices were hoarse from conversation. There was something so *real* about connecting with another human being on a soul-level; there were no boundaries between us— love and friendship had destroyed them. I walked away from the experience changed, and even the dumpster full of our house's beer cans looked beautiful as I contemplated how I could have more experiences like that one. How could church compete with that? When had I ever left church undeniably, beautifully changed? All too often, I sang "Just As I Am," and left just as I was.

As I came to understand my experiences with my fraternity at the University of Tennessee as having something to do with the sacred, and as I studied Scripture with a campus faith community, I found this search for deep, personal connections to be one that others have shared. After all, we celebrate Communion in the form of a *shared* meal that breaks down boundaries between rich and poor, male and female, Jews and Greeks. Time and again, Christians read in the Bible that one of the places we experience God is in the faces of *other people*—in the poor, the marginalized, even fraternity brothers who stay up too late playing beer pong. It was this gradual understanding that God had more to do with people and less to do with individual salvation, which prompted my faith to shift in new and exciting ways.

Scripture came alive as I began to see it as a book of questions, not a book of answers, and I began to actually converse with the text. Never before had I seen Scripture as something that was written by people, with all their imperfections. To my astonishment, the authors of a holy book were the sick and the lame, the loved and the needy. Instead of seeing Scripture as a book of rules—staid and rigid—the Bible became a campfire. People throughout the centuries have gathered around this campfire to ask the tough questions about God, humanity, and everything else. I realized that I was a part of that legacy, and that how I answered the questions presented in the text *mattered*. I had to undertake the difficult task of determining what made something a *good* answer, because Scripture was not as univocal as I had been made to believe.

So instead of asking, "Does this have scriptural grounding?" and assuming that there was a clear-cut answer to be found, I began to ask another question: "What does this *do* to people who are beloved by God?" These different questions have led to different answers than I would have given before becoming a brother of the Chi Phi fraternity. For instance, where I had before held a typical evangelical view of LGBTQ people (love the sinner, hate the sin), I began to advocate for broader inclusion within the church. Because, as I talked to some of my brothers, both out and closeted, about these issues, I began to understand just how devastating an approach I was taking. These were more than friends, they were my brothers, and more importantly, they were the beloved of God. Who was I to turn them away or condemn them?

Suddenly all the hard stances that I took in the past began to melt away before my eyes, and before I knew it, I found myself in situations I had never dreamed of, protesting around issues of worker justice and working for the inclusion of LGBTQ people in churches. Of course, my brothers were not the only force in my life that helped me make that shift—my progressive faith community dedicated to reading Scripture together, for instance, was very important—but my brothers were the catalyst. As odd as it sounds, my world had been changed by some guys in their twenties who drank like fish and swore like sailors.

Living in the Chi Phi house also taught me that communal life is messy and best lived in covenant. My brothers and I were bound by a set of oaths we took to one another and we affirmed those oaths through our creed, which we said at our weekly meetings. In that creed we promise to protect one another from harm, be there for one another, and uphold the triple-values of truth, honor, and personal integrity. In doing so, we proclaim that nearly two hundred years later, there are still people who "believe in the Chi Phi fraternity." Our joint belief in one another and the structure of our community bound us together in covenant, and that safety allowed us to be frank and honest with one another.

My fraternity, like most fraternities at the University of Tennessee, was overwhelmingly conservative, so when I shared with them my evolving religious and social views, they often vehemently disagreed. Yet, because we shared a sense of community, this did not drive us apart. In the churches I grew up in, membership was based on holding a certain set of doctrines to be true, but my brothers' model for community was different. It was a breath of fresh air. My brothers showed me that community was not about assent, but about providing the kind of spaces where disagreement and doubt are welcome. In a strange way, inebriated conversations with my best friends taught me what church is supposed to look like—love, discussion, and covenant. After having spent my college years participating in and helping to build a community like this, I have no desire to go back to how things used to be.

My call to ministry looks different than it did before Chi Phi. Instead of focusing on being a *pastor*, I instead see myself as exploring a dual-vocation in *community building* and *storytelling*. In essence, I want to help provide spaces for people to be transformed as I was. I want to put people in situations where they can stare into the eyes of other human beings and see the very light of God looking back at them. I want to help people realize that Jesus is with them in prayer and at church, but Jesus is also with them at the supermarket, in the subway, and at work.

Living with my brothers, I came to believe we are all storytellers; the question is what kind of story we are telling. Will our stories empower or deplete, create or destroy, work for justice or oppression? These stories shape human beings and how they perceive the world. Our stories matter. If our story tells us that God is not concerned with people who are different from us, then we will not experience God in those places. As the saying goes, "the size of your lens is the size of your God." Storytelling and community building then are ways to enlarge our lens, allowing us to see God in new places—like a rundown frat house in between campus and an infamous row of bars. Maybe God lives there, too, if we are not too busy to search.

Before joining a fraternity, I thought that it was all about huge parties with kegs of beer and the occasional philanthropy event. Little did I know that Chi Phi was really about people—my brothers, the brothers at the University of Tennessee who graduated before me and after me, and the brothers from thousands of miles away and two hundred years ago. The sense of feeling connected to other human beings was inexorably spiritual, and it was spiritual in a different way than I had experienced in churches. At its core, it challenged everything I thought I knew about God, church, Scripture, faith, doubt, and politics. My faith had been centered on facts and fancy words like *atonement* and *hypostatic union*, but now it focuses on communities of individuals. Who would have thought that walking into candlelit rooms, dressing in colorful robes, and living in a rundown house with my closest friends would be the thing that finally got me to understand what the "body of Christ" looks like? But it was there on frat row where I found God anew.

QUESTIONS FOR DISCUSSION:

1. Woolf writes that life in his fraternity changed the way he experienced faith and read the Bible. He stopped looking for *you singular* and started learning to appreciate a community of brothers. How might more fraternities, sororities, and other residence life support a similar experience for others? How might they model community?
2. Discuss Woolf's essays with stereotypes of fraternities in mind. What connections or surprises surfaced?

16

THREE PARTIES

Lauren Deidra Sawyer

I.

It's my first college party, and I'm graduating in three days. The counter is full of brightly colored booze bottles, lemons, shot glasses. The blue bottles are vodka; those warmer oranges, scotch and whiskey. Ben brought hard cider. Kate made Sex on the Beach, a fruity concoction with orange juice, peach schnapps, vodka.

We're all communications students—soon-to-be-graduates, that is—from our small Christian college. We've spent four years quietly disobeying our university's alcohol ban; this is the first time someone is brave enough to throw a party. Under the guise of a Bible study, no less. We tell each other, tipsy in just fifteen minutes, how we should have done this sooner. Like, four years sooner.

I find myself on the front porch with the smokers. I'm protected here with them. The smokers' porch: an introvert's safe zone. I'm standing with the prettiest girl in college, who married the hottest guy in college. They both work at the coffee shop on campus, the one that has an unspoken "you must be *this* good looking" qualification for hire. She's next to a skater kid and Kaleigh, a theater major, whom I've only spoken to in passing.

I share smokes to make friends.

"I really only smoke at gay bars," Kaleigh tells me. I teach her how to light her cig. "So I'm not very good at it."

By mentioning gay bars at all, Kaleigh opens the conversation to a favorite topic for us "worldly" communications majors—homosexuality. Our evangelical university takes a certain position, one it would indubitably call "The Christian Response to Homosexuality," supposedly a memo from Jesus himself: "It is Wrong to Be Gay." And if your kid or uncle or brother's gay: Pray Away the Gay.

But we comm majors think differently. We consider ourselves the most "liberal" of the majors, fully embracing the liberal-media stereotype given to us by Fox News. We comm majors know a few of our peers are gay, but they're forced to keep quiet. If the university finds out that they're gay, especially a *practicing* homosexual, they could be reprimanded: counseling, suspension, expulsion.

"I hate that there are always labels," Kaleigh says to me. "Like, if I fall in love with someone, that's what I am." She tells me that she has made out with a few girls, but has never fallen in love. I wonder what my school would say about her behavior; it certainly would not comply with our "healthy boundaries" training.

"I think we like to categorize things too much, to make ourselves feel safe," I say. "If we can label you, then we don't need to get to know you." I'm a bit of a sage while I'm drunk. Hannah, the host, comes outside with sparklers. Kaleigh and I become distracted and our conversation ends.

Later, after some sobering up, I sit on the porch with my friends Mallory and Rachel, smoking. Rachel's smoking her first ever. Mallory, her second. The three of us, new, social-smokers, feel cool. Deviant. We practice our exhales, trying to make rings, but not knowing how.

I started smoking out of rebellion—against my boyfriend Nate. We broke up, temporarily, the previous winter. Many of our arguments were over smoking: how I hated it, how I wish he wouldn't do it. This was not so puritanical of me to think this, though. I wasn't exercising my good Christian morals. I think a part of me was jealous that a tiny cylinder of paper and tobacco got more attention than me sometimes. Four days after we split, I bought my first pack. I've been a pack-a-month girl ever since.

I wonder, sometimes, if my sexual activity with Nate came out of rebellion against God or my school, the way I had rebelled against our breakup by smoking. Maybe, subconsciously, I was making a point, like premarital sex doesn't screw up future marriages; neither does it keep you out of heaven. (I've heard these lines so often.) But when it comes down to it, when he and I are together, kissing, then more, then more, then more, I don't feel like I am rebelling against anything. I feel just the opposite.

But still, the guilt weighs my belly down with bricks. I don't tell anyone what Nate and I are doing. Though with my friends, drinking may be acceptable, cigarettes, too, I fear I must have crossed the line with this bad-girl behavior.

I didn't always carry these guilt bricks with me. In high school, I hardly had a reason to. I was the star Sunday school student: I could beat anyone in a round of Bible trivia and was the first to offer a benediction prayer at the end of the hour. I tried so hard to be perfect; and it seemed that by my senior year, I had mastered it.

That is, until that spring in the parking lot of a Starbucks, when my best friend came out to me. We sat in my car, holding iced mochas and napkins between our thighs.

"I'm gay," she said. "Well, bisexual." No need for build-up. She went on to explain why she was jealous of my boyfriends, why she always wanted me around. She *liked* me.

"No, I don't think that's it," I argued. "We're just best friends." I thought of all the times we slept in each other's bed, how we changed clothes in front of each other. I no longer craved my frothy drink. I practiced my best Christian face: a half-smile my eyes didn't match. They were wide, I was sure, and on the verge of tearing up.

My practice in being good had not prepared me for this. I believed there was a clear line between what was good (being straight) and what was bad (being anything but straight). So my response to her, that "No, I don't think you are attracted to me," was really, "No, I don't think you are gay." I wanted so much for her to be on the "good" side with me; I wasn't ready to give her up to the "bad." Either way, our friendship ended soon after that.

Off to college in the fall, I expected to blend in with my fellow Christian classmates. But as perfect as I saw myself, everyone around me seemed just *that* much more perfect. In my classes and mandatory chapel, we were told how by the power of Christ and lots and lots of effort, we could manage to be free of any *intentional* sin. I could tell I was falling behind, but by then I doubted that perfection was even worth my time. After all, it had lost me a best friend.

Then my sophomore year, in a chapel series on sexuality, I met those guilt bricks head-on. The speakers, two pastors brought in from some megachurch, reintroduced that good/bad polarity: *Do* make sure you date a devoted Christian. And, *don't* kiss him when the lights are off.

I felt sick to my stomach, guilty—guilty that there was a part of me that might, one day, want to kiss a boy again, lights on or off.

The next year when Nate and I started dating and we found ourselves breaking the chapel speakers' rules and more, I felt so bad I couldn't pick up my Bible without crying. I started asking myself, *What is wrong with me? How did I go from being a good girl to bad?* The only things that kept me from being pummeled by those bricks were months of counseling, anxiety pills, and quietly ignoring everything I had learned from Christians about sex.

II.

With graduation now two days away, this is party number two.

We're in the corner of the bar, behind the bathrooms, the fans blowing smoke from anywhere farther right. On our table: the beers we ordered. Rachel's been playing around with my cigarette case. Mallory fingers my lighter. My artist friend Keith is joining us for this party, since he missed last night's. It was his idea. Beatniks is Keith's place, the only bar in town that someone under 40 could frequent and feel cool. He tells us he spent all last summer here for the free Wi-Fi and the cheap Guinness.

The last time the five of us went to a bar together was four months ago, just before spring semester started. We all serve on the newspaper staff—except Mallory, who lives with Rachel—and we wanted one last hurrah before worrying about a second semester's worth of evasive sources, stubborn administrators, our pain-in-the-ass adviser.

Then, we drove to Muncie, Indiana, a city known for little. Outside the Midwest, few have even heard of it. For those of us stuck in the Corn Belt, we know Muncie as the home of Ball State University and several cool bars. It also happens to be far enough from our own campus that we feel safe drinking publicly. I took my friends to the bar Nate loves—it's decorated like a Beowulfian epic, bras dangling from elk antlers. At this point, Nate and I were still on a break. Part of me wanted to go to make him jealous. So I sent him a text, telling him where I was. When he seemed unimpressed, I texted him a penis joke to see how he would feel about *that*.

He didn't like it much.

"I don't want to hear you say that. It's crass."

It was crass. Frankly, talking about *his* penis to him or anyone else is crass, crude, and cheap. I just wanted to rile him up, to show him that I was a bold girl, to show him that he isn't the only person I could fool around with. (The guilt bricks lightened with beer.) The truth is, at the end of those two months apart, I couldn't picture myself with any other guy, not even holding hands, let alone getting it on. I believed Nate and I were what the Bible calls "one flesh." I couldn't separate myself from him. Not that I wanted to.

Two and a half drinks later, I didn't care about Nate at all. At least, his text, "Let's hang out soon," was promising enough. Plus the game of drunk Trivial Pursuit Jack and I had begun was too fun.

"Wait, wait! I know this: Alaska. No, Antarctica!"

On Nate's and my first date, he gave me a tour of my hometown. We went to my favorite restaurants and coffee shops, my favorite parks, mall, and ice cream shop. The date lasted fifteen hours; at hour ten, blushing, Nate asked to hold my hand.

Now we spend our dates at South Side, the smoky diner in the middle of our college town. Something in the murky near-coffee and stained booths draws conversation out of us. Here we can talk for hours about our favorite -ologies—about cosmology, technology, and, some-times, theology. The text I received from Nate that winter night at the Muncie bar—"Let's hang out soon"—was the text that led us to South Side the next day, where after an eleven-hour date, our two-month hiatus ended and we got back together.

Back at Beatniks: "When are you going to tell me?" I whisper to Jack, who's sitting across from me. He is the one who doesn't remember anything from last night, from party number one. A lightweight. After two shots he had "bullshit" stamped on his belly. (Jack: "How'd it get there?" Rachel: "That was me, honey. I wanted to test the stamp.")

Jack looks nervous. As news editor, I've never seen him this way. He's confident, egotistical, the perfect newspaper man. "Tonight? Now?" he asks. Jack looks for when the rest of the group is distracted, and he pulls our hands together, to hide the whisper. "I date boys." I sigh relief: he's my favorite friend to touch. Hand to arm, hand to back, chest to chest. I touch his knuckles. "Interesting."

III.

We graduated today, so we buy our alcohol in town, shamelessly. I posted on Rachel's Facebook a few hours earlier: "I'm bringing stuff for White Russians! Mmm!" Even then I feel a little guilty about who might see the post. I reprimand myself, "Hey, it's OK to drink now, remember?" What a difference a day makes.

We're all here at Rachel's place, a cute cottage-style house just a block from campus. We're drinking Sex on the Beach, our new favorite cocktail, when Keith gets a text from his housemate Stephen, the former student body president of our college. He wants to come and drink for the very first time.

Keith and I leave to pick up Stephen and go on a booze run. I haven't found Kahlúa for my White Russians and Keith wants enough beer to play a game he learned from a television show, one in which everyone shares a bottle of whiskey and at least one case of beer. No one is really set on playing the game, but he insists a game will be the only way to get Stephen to drink. So off we go.

On the way to the Save-On across town ("They have the best selection!"), Keith jokes about seeing me through the windows at Nate's house, which is across an alleyway from his and Stephen's place. He knows I'm staying with Nate for a few days before heading back home for summer break.

I reply, "Nah, Nate's room is in the front of the house. You'll never see me."

"Wait, you stay in his room?"

Caught off guard, I use my best defense: "Don't judge!"

"Oh, I'm not."

I wonder what Stephen, precious little Stephen, is thinking. He worked with Nate last summer; he loves and respects my boyfriend, maybe because they're so different. Stephen is sweet, dorky, a sociable guy. Nate is tough, private, an introvert. No matter how confident I pretend to be in my decision to disregard this whole "premarital sex will send you to hell" thing—I can't deny my nature. I feel guilt strongly. I think, "Stephen, don't judge me."

When we get home with forty-eight bottles of beer and my on-sale bottle of Kahlúa, we play a drinking game: the card game War, with certain rules. If you lose a war with someone, you take a shot. If you play the same number as someone else, but don't war, you take a shot. If you lay a Jack, the last person to touch his nose loses and takes a shot. After a few rounds of our theater-major friend taking all the shots, we change the rules: only when you lose war do you take a shot. You just take a drink of beer with everything else.

Most of us are sufficiently tipsy by the end of the game. Sweet little Stephen decided against shots and took only sips of his Blue Moon instead.

Jack lies on the couch alone, and I come up to him, sitting and pulling my legs to my chest. "How ya doin'?"

He says he's fine, that he's just texting. But I wonder if he's had too much, like our theater major friend who looks sickly. The two of them had taken most of the shots once we instigated a new rule: if you speak with an accent, you take a shot. Jack found a way to break out into a British, Russian, or pirate accent much too often. He's paying for it. Drunk Jack is in confession-mode still.

"You know my friend Isaac from L.A.?"

"Yeah, I think so."

"We dated." This makes sense, I think. I remember Jack bringing up Isaac occasionally at newspaper meetings, when we're hanging out. *So they were a thing!*

A few weeks later Jack would tell me the whole story: the time when he first started finding himself attracted to boys, when he first kissed one, dated one. His guilt, excitement, and fear. That night we talked about the Kinsey scale, about how attraction is not black-and-white, but rather more of a spectrum. I wonder what other things could be on a spectrum, other things not so clear.

QUESTIONS FOR DISCUSSION:

1. The essay considers the topic of rebellion in several different ways. How can rebelling against university rules, theological claims, or expected communal practices affect one's faith and life?

2. It's popular to critique college partying culture but, in Sawyer's case, the three parties seem to be places for thoughtful discovery. What's the best role for partying and drinking in college?

17

FAITH TRANSFORMS IN TIMES OF CRISIS

Br. Lawrence A. Whitney

INTRODUCTION[1]

Going to college is supposed to be a time of finding yourself—figuring out who you really are, discovering what makes you come alive, experimenting with alternate ways of being and doing, finding the pieces of yourself and integrating them. Some of this existential peregrination, this personal wandering, happens in the classroom, where possibilities for self-actualization, amongst other things, can be explored and critically examined in a controlled environment. Much of it happens, though, in the dorms, dining halls, athletic fields, theater stages, student unions, and occasionally even the campus chapel, all of which provide greater freedom to be entrepreneurial and experimental.

Unfortunately, on occasion events transpire to scatter the pieces of themselves that students have managed to find and appropriate. Such incidents transgress the bounds of safety and force students to cope with violation and loss. The transgression may be interpersonal, communal, or even regional, national, or global in scope. As the pieces fall apart it can feel as if a limb has been torn from the body, or even as though the whole body has been dismembered, just as too many victims of such transgressions experience carnally. In these instances, the work of ministry is to help campus communities remember, and thereby

---

1. Parts of this chapter are taken from the sermon "Re-Membering" preached by the author at Marsh Chapel, Boston University, on Sunday, May 26, 2013 and available at http://blogs.bu.edu/sermons/2013/05/26/re-membering/.

re-member, what was lost. This is the ministry of empowerment to move forward in life, not in spite of the eruption of tragedy, grief, and loss, but having embraced, balanced, and carried it.

9/11

The second Tuesday of my freshman year of college some people flew two airplanes into each of the towers of the World Trade Center in New York and another into the Pentagon in Washington, D.C. I was safely ensconced at Ithaca College, on South Hill overlooking Lake Cayuga in the Finger Lakes region of upstate New York. I was four hours from Manhattan and six hours from home, just outside Washington in Silver Spring, Maryland. But I did not feel safe. My naïve sense that the United States is a universally admired country was instantly and starkly proven wrong. My experience growing up in one of the most religiously diverse parts of the United States was that people of diverse faiths can and do live together harmoniously. This perception was similarly proven desperately naïve. And the response of the United States, to attack Afghanistan, made the least sense of all.

I attended the interfaith vigil on campus, where we prayed together for peace. I listened to Karen Armstrong attempt to explain the motivations to violence among fundamentalist religious groups in a campus lecture. I participated in conversations with friends and classmates and faculty and staff. We attempted to make sense of what happened and why it impacted us so deeply. I immersed myself in music making. This was the reason I had decided to attend Ithaca College, after all: to major in music. All of these things were helpful to some degree and in various ways. But none of them satisfied the deep sense of violation and loss that accompanied this truly global event. It cast into sharp relief precisely how broken and fragmented our world really is. I had to entirely rethink my worldview.

Andrew Fitz-Gibbon offered to host a Eucharist for peace and healing in Muller Chapel. He was teaching sociology at IC at the time and was a priest in an ecumenical Christian community. The Protestant Chaplain, the Rev. Dr. Allison Stokes, encouraged me to attend. I went, mainly because I was available and Allison had suggested it, not because I thought much of anything was actually going to help by that point.

Strangely, it did help. It did so in the same way the Eucharist always does: by telling over and over again the story of Jesus. Of course, healing and peacemaking are central to that story. This telling is a special kind of remembering, an anamnesis. In this telling and retelling, our remembering of God's dismemberment in the crucifixion of Jesus is held together with our own brokenness. Our remembering of God's re-memberment in the resurrection of Jesus is held together with our own desire for healing. The invitation to the Eucharistic table is an invitation to participate in the dismemberment and re-memberment of God.

No matter how little sense the attack on 9/11 made, and how little sense the U.S. response made, there is a message and experience of hope available in a life of faith that transcends reason and sensibility. I had always enjoyed communion growing up in Hughes United Methodist Church, but I never really understood it or experienced it at the depths of the life of faith until that day. Meeting Andy and participating in that Eucharistic experience was the beginning of a spiritual journey that I could never have imagined at the time, but that has become absolutely central to who I am and how I live my life. Over the next four years I explored that ecumenical Christian community Andy leads and discovered that Christian life and faith is far more about disciplined practice, such as regular Eucharistic participation, than it is about right belief. I was noviced and professed in the Lindisfarne Community, and later ordained to the diaconate and then the priesthood. This is why my students at Boston University know me as Brother Larry.

PATRIOTS' DAY 2013

The day was just a little warmer than the runners may have wanted, but perfect for spectators who came out in droves to line the course of the Boston Marathon, particularly the last few miles as the runners came down Beacon Street, through Kenmore Square, and then zigged and zagged over to Boylston Street to the finish line. My dean, the Rev. Dr. Robert Allan Hill, is a runner, and so he hosts an annual Marathon Monday brunch of eggs and fruit and Dunkin Donuts in his residence in Kenmore Square. Dean Hill recited Longfellow and the Gettysburg Address, as he is wont to do sometimes. Out we processed to Kenmore

Square to watch the elite runners come through, thinking that we were only taking our lives in our hands by boarding the rickety elevator.

How little did we know. My wife and I walked from Kenmore Square back home and I lay down to take a nap. I detest being rudely awoken from a sound sleep. When Holly shook my shoulder and announced, "There are bombs at the marathon!" all I could think was, "That's ridiculous. Bombs don't belong at marathons!" I looked at my phone: missed calls, missed texts, missed e-mail. We called our parents. "I have to get to the chapel," I announced. "How?" my wife inquired. Good question. How do you get from Beacon Hill to Boston University without going anywhere near Copley Square? Thank God for Hubway, Boston's brand new bike sharing system! I grabbed a bike, carried it over to the Esplanade, and rode hard.

It turns out that when you stop a race before it is completed and throw the runners off the course, life gets a bit confusing for everyone. Runners came over to Commonwealth Avenue from Beacon Street, many of them hoping to catch the T, only to find that the T was shut down. What did they find? A church! Boston University's Marsh Chapel. In they came and hospitality we provided: water, food, blankets, phones, rides, directions, counsel, prayer, patience. We planned a vigil for that evening. News broke that there was an explosion at the JFK library. We cancelled the vigil. The vigil finally happened the following evening and hundreds gathered on Marsh Plaza in front of the chapel for readings, and prayers, and words of comfort and strength in times of trouble. Soon, we gathered in the nave of Marsh Chapel for readings, prayers, sermon, song, hymns, and Eucharist as we continued the search for healing.

"Is there a student at Boston University named Lu Lingzi?" Dean Hill asked. I typed her name into the computer. "Yes." "Oh." Lingzi was no longer missing. She was at the morgue. One of the three killed by the bombings. The media frenzy was intense as the news broke. Over four hundred students, most of them Chinese, gathered in the Burke Room at Agganis Arena to share memories and process together. Her parents arrived from China and were greeted at the airport by the Ambassador from China and a delegation from Boston University. Fourteen hundred people, including many dignitaries, gathered in the George Sherman Union for Lingzi's memorial service. Four thousand watched a live stream over the Internet. In the course of a morning,

$560,000 was gathered by the Trustees of Boston University to begin a scholarship fund in her memory. Her father gave a poignant and moving eulogy. Her mother was inconsolable.

On the Thursday following the attack I helped pick up the mother and cousin of a student who was injured in the bombing at the airport. We got them to the hospital and then to the hotel and were just getting ready to head home when we heard that an MIT police officer had been shot. After I finally arrived home, I spent most of the night and most of the next day, riveted to Twitter as the lockdown of the greater Boston area played out while the police tracked down the two men who, it turned out, were responsible for the bombings earlier in the week. Intermittently, I joined conference calls and responded to e-mail as we sought to comfort the anxieties of our students who were locked up in their dorm rooms.

A number of students I spoke with in the immediate aftermath of the bombings did not quite identify with the sense of terror so many were experiencing. In fact, they were struggling to figure out exactly what they did feel. These students had a sense of being at BU, not so much in Boston more generally, and so they felt somewhat distanced from what had transpired only a few blocks away in Copley Square. For students, faculty, and staff who were running in the marathon, watching the end of the race on Boylston Street, or helping in the medical tents, the experience was decidedly different.

Marathon Monday at Boston University is recognized nationally as one of the top collegiate "events" that bond students to each other and to the institution. This year, the marathon inspired disillusion and dislocation. In particular, those who had worked in the medical tents expressed a deep sense that they would never be able to experience the world quite the same way again. After all, they had prepared to aid people whose legs were cramped or strained, not to treat people who no longer had any legs at all.

The Friday lockdown of the city brought many of those who had felt more aloof from the events of Marathon Monday into the cohort of the existentially dismembered. You know something is wrong when dining services is delivering bagged lunches to the dorm so that you do not have to risk a venture outside.

Ministry in the wake of these events was the hard work of listening to those who were involved in the events of Patriots' Day, attending to those who felt violated by the lockdown during the manhunt, and facilitating meetings and services for people to gather and feel the strength of being together in community. This work of helping a community to reconstruct a sense of trust and dependability together is a process of accompanying individuals and groups as they remember and thus re-member themselves and each other. Important to exercising this type of ministry well is letting go of the need to know which moment and manner of accompaniment, if any, served as a turning point for any given person. The ministry of facilitation I carried out in Boston was exactly the same ministry provided for me at Ithaca College in the wake of 9/11.

Lingzi's parents buried her here in Boston. They did so because they believe that her spirit will help to bring peace to our community. Lingzi's family's having entrusted her body and spirit to the city is a sign that it is in fact possible to be and feel safe in the wake of acts of terror.

BINLAND LEE

The phone rang. "Brother Larry, I know it's Sunday morning and you have services, but there has been a fire, and a student has died, and several are in the hospital. Can you go to the hospital?" More death. More trauma. Binland Lee was a senior in the Marine Science program at the College of Arts and Sciences at Boston University. She was well-known on campus, much beloved for her compassion and free spirit, and admired for her intellect and optimism. The fire broke out at 6:30 a.m. and destroyed the three-story house where she lived with eighteen other people, including several other BU students. When I arrived at the hospital, as an official of the University I could not yet confirm that Binland was the one fatality in the fire, but her friends knew. One of them was under the impression that she would be able to get back into her apartment to retrieve some belongings, and it was a careful process to explain that there simply was nothing to go back to. Only two short weeks before graduation, the confidence that they would all go on to be happy and successful was gone in the wake of their own lives being ravaged and the life of their friend being torn away.

I accompanied a group of students down to Brooklyn for Binland's wake and memorial service. Her family is Chinese Buddhist, and the service reflected the traditions of Chinese Buddhism, even as they were enacted in the context of an Italian Catholic funeral home. It was a perfect example of the juxtapositions that constitute religious pluralism in the United States these days. Several of the students were unclear about how to participate. I encouraged them to simply observe what members of her family were doing and, as they felt comfortable or were invited, to follow suit. Several students asked questions about what was actually happening. Most I was equipped to answer, but in response to a few of the questions I had to shrug my shoulders and say, "I don't know, but the most important thing is to be respectful." In Chinese religion, to be respectful is to be faithful.

Going down to Brooklyn was hard, not only because it was right on the heels of addressing the Boston Marathon bombing and its after-math, but also because I knew very well what they were going through, and accompanying them brought back some hard memories.

LINDA TRINH

On January 23, 2005, my high school friend and classmate Linda Trinh was sexually assaulted and murdered in her Baltimore apartment. Her roommate found her dead, face down in the bath tub, dressed only from the waist up, with a bruise on the left side of her face. She had been asphyxiated. It took a while, but the police eventually caught the perpetrator of this heinous crime and he was convicted and sentenced to a very long prison term.

Linda was a senior biomedical engineering major, on the volleyball team, and president of her sorority. She was conducting research on making mammography more affordable in the developing world so that people could get breast cancer screenings. When she visited her native Vietnam the previous summer with her father, Linda worked at an AIDS orphanage for a month. She had a passion for making the world a better place through the intelligence and talents with which God graced her. She had a heart of loving compassion for everyone.

I was a senior at Ithaca College when it happened. The next day I was headed into a meeting when I got a call from my friend Cory. "Do you remember Linda Trinh?" he asked. "Of course." "She's dead." As he explained what happened I was in shock. I hung up and shook my head, and I remember the fleeting thought that this could not be real. I went into the meeting, but part way through I stood up, threw my Gatorade bottle against the wall, and walked out the door, much to the shock and consternation of many of my friends.

Cory and I drove home together for the funeral. We speculated about who among our high school friends would be there. We talked around Linda a lot; it was too hard to talk about her. That night was the viewing. It was open casket. People showed up in droves. Linda's parents were beside themselves with grief. Everyone talked in whispers; we were all in shock. There were many tears.

The next day was the funeral. Linda was Catholic so they had a full funeral mass. There was a slight twist, however. Her parents immigrated to the United States from Vietnam in 1983 to escape persecution from the communist government and to find a better life for their family, and so they are members of a Vietnamese Catholic church. The entire mass was in Vietnamese. In some ways this turned out to be a good thing. The religious diversity of our high school spanned people involved in myriad forms of Christianity, and also included Jews, Hindus, Sikhs, Muslims, and Buddhists, just to name a few. The fact that the service was in Vietnamese allowed us to pray together without content getting in the way, as we did not understand what was said. After the funeral, there was a motorcade that stretched for miles to the cemetery. At the graveside, after a few words from the priest, the casket was lowered into the ground, and everyone threw flowers into the grave. It was one of the hardest things I have ever done. I was twenty-one years old; I should not have been burying my friend.

CONCLUSION

In the wake of so much crisis and tragedy, thanks be to God, there is hope. The Christian doctrine of the trinity is fundamentally the belief that God in Godself is a community of members. One of those members became incarnate in Jesus Christ and was thus, for a time, dismembered from God, and so God knows the pain of dismemberment as God experienced the pain of the passion. And yet, God also knows the healing and joy of re-membering in the glory of the resurrection. It is the work of remembering this re-membering that goes on in the Eucharist.

Furthermore, as faithful people remember these events of tragedy, there is hope that we may be re-membered together with those who have died and, as hard as it may be to imagine, with those who perpetrated the events leading to the tragedy in the first place. Accompaniment in my own process of re-membering was the ministry provided to me in times of crisis, and I have sought to provide this ministry to others as a chaplain. The work of ministry on a college or university campus is often the work of helping a community to remember, and thus to re-member.

QUESTIONS FOR DISCUSSION:

1. What tragedies have affected your journey and/or your community during college?
2. What does the author mean by "re-membering"? What might re-membering look and feel like to you?

Section V

Studying Off-Campus, Studying Within

What comes to mind when we think of the stereotypical college study? Perhaps, it's students reading on a grassy quadrangle. Or, late night study sessions in dormitories. Many also think of a semester's study abroad, often occurring in a student's junior year.

In our nation's top colleges and universities, study abroad is fairly common, but it's rather unusual at other schools. While the number of U.S. students studying abroad in recent years has increased, according to the Open Doors 2013 report of the Institute of International Education, about 9 percent of students study abroad before graduation. During the 2011–2012 academic year, about 1 percent of students enrolled at institutions of higher education were abroad. Those who do travel internationally take questions of faith and college with them to new cultural contexts. Others—indeed, most students at colleges and universities—study off-campus in one way or another; it's just not for college credit. Many have summer jobs or internships where they can earn money and learn the ways of the world. Some students take service learning courses that include experiences at local non-profits or businesses. Classrooms remain important, but much of college learning occurs a long way from the quadrangle.

In Section V, readers will encounter four such stories of studying off-campus. Andrea Campo, in "Christians Suffer from Depression, Too," describes her journey from a community college to a church-related college, but it was in Spain that her faith was most tested. Johnna Purchase went to a college program in Ireland where an Irish classmate won her heart. Purchase's essay on God's part in this is, "The Dating Game: God, Ireland, and One Woman of Little Faith." Writing about his experience at one of the nation's most respected historically black colleges, Edward Anderson's "Death and Life" examines his journey to navigate his family's faith and a summer spent in the inner city. Finally, in an appropriately titled concluding essay, "Strange Benediction," Joseph Paillé relates how a summer spent working in Yellowstone National Park changed his life's direction (and his musical repertoire).

The Christian faith calls us to learn and serve beyond the walls of any institution—college, church, or otherwise. Clearly, students' college experiences should never be confined to a classroom or library. These pages inspire us, and give us courage, to journey from campus to follow God's calling wherever that may lead.

18

CHRISTIANS SUFFER FROM DEPRESSION, TOO

Andrea Campo

If there's one thing I learned from attending Calvin College, a small Christian liberal arts college in Grand Rapids, Michigan, it's that a diploma only tells part of the story. In college I learned that, even at a Christian school, Christians aren't immune to the many challenges of life. I've seen fellow twentysomethings get divorced, struggle with addictions, face ostracism from their loved ones because of their sexuality, and lose their faith in God. As I watch them in the midst of their trials, they watch me as I figure out how to reconcile my faith with the fact that I suffer from depression.

After graduating from high school, I settled into a life that was decidedly less exciting than I wanted it to be. I opted to attend community college before Calvin as a way to save money. While my friends were having the time of their lives living away from home and savoring new freedoms, I was still living with my parents and sitting through core classes that were laughably easy. My brain knew it was temporary, but my heart felt that this "temporary" was going to last forever. As the semester progressed, it got harder to get out of bed in the morning and easier to contemplate death. It wasn't that I wanted to die, exactly; I just didn't see the point in living anymore.

At first, I didn't tell anyone how I was feeling because I didn't want people to feel sorry for me. A casual observer would have said that there was really no good reason for me to feel the way I did. My life had been free of tragedy: no one close to me had ever died; I had never experienced any sort of trauma; my parents were still married to each other. Plus, most importantly, I was a Christian. Throughout my childhood I had been told that Christians weren't supposed to get depressed because we have God in our hearts. "Christians have been showered with so many blessings from God and whenever they feel sad, they should just focus on the blessings and they'll feel better," said a former Sunday school teacher of mine.

After about six months of battling that crippling sadness, I got used to thinking of my condition as depression. I read online about the symptoms of depression and I took a handful of questionnaires on Calvin's Counseling Center's website that helped students self-assess for depression. Even though I'd reached a better understanding of what was happening in my brain, I still didn't want anyone to know about it for fear that I would be judged.

Eventually, fatigue from fighting alone overcame my fear of facing judgment. One by one, I told my secret to my closest friends. I started to let people in. They listened. They understood. To my great relief, they *accepted* me. Bolstered by their encouragement, I started working up the courage to tell my parents and ask for their help. I had a terrible feeling that they wouldn't believe me. I feared that I would somehow have to convince them of something that I myself sometimes had trouble believing. In fact, every time someone urged me to talk to my parents, I was afraid of being rejected. I had to continually give the excuse that it wasn't worth it because they wouldn't believe me anyway.

When I finally told my parents that I thought I was depressed, my mother's exact words were, "It's probably just seasonal. You just need to exercise more and it will go away." Did she simply not believe me? Or, did she not want to believe her daughter was wrestling with an invisible illness? Either way, I felt crushed by her dismissal even as it justified my reticence to talk to my parents in the first place. My expectations had been fulfilled, so I promised myself that I would never talk to them about it again since, I convinced myself, I already knew what they would say. I began to seek further support from friends and other adults in my life. Now, years later, I think I understand my mom's reaction more fully. No mother wants to hear that her child is unhappy and doesn't know how to change that. Ignoring the condition—as I had tried to do for many months—seems like a reasonable response. But, I learned, it wasn't enough.

After accruing as many core class credits as possible at the community college, I transferred to Calvin halfway through my sophomore year. One year later, as a junior, I boarded a plane bound for my semester abroad in Spain. While I was there, my mental and emotional health reached an all-time low. I was away from friends, family, and my entire support system. Of the twenty-four Calvin students in the program, I knew only two people when we left the United States. I was living with a host family that spoke no English and it took us a long time to get used to each other. I didn't even want to be in Spain in the first place, but with a semester abroad, I could complete my Spanish Education major. I ended up failing one of my classes due, in large part, to the worsening of my depression. Failing was a first for me. I had always managed to pull decent grades despite my lack of focus and general apathy toward life, but there I was, failing a class that I actually needed in order to graduate.

That was a pretty horrible day. After receiving my final exam with the 52 percent on it, I trudged back to my host family's apartment, my mind spinning wildly through all the possible outcomes of this failed class: I'd have to take it over, that was a given. What would my friends say? What would my parents say? Would they be disappointed? Would I get in trouble?

As I walked, my thoughts turned darker: Was this a sign that I should leave Spain and go back home? Should I even bother to stay for the rest of my courses? What if I failed more classes? Would I be able to keep going? I'm miserable. Is it worth it to even be alive?

It might seem melodramatic and highly illogical to be suicidal after failing a class. People fail things every day. It's not the end of the world. But here's the thing: depression isn't logical. It wasn't failing the class that made me want to kill myself. Instead, that failure emphasized all my other feelings of failure. It represented my failure as a person. Failure to be happy, failure to cope, failure to be a good Christian. It was just too hard and I couldn't do it anymore.

I got out of bed, where I had sought refuge, and walked out onto the balcony. The sky looked as if a storm was brewing just beyond the horizon, which was the way I often felt. I gripped the railing of the balcony and rocked back and forth with my stomach resting on the metal bar. My apartment was five stories up and a headfirst dive off the balcony would surely kill me. It wasn't that I desperately wanted to be dead, but I couldn't think of any good reasons to stay alive. I felt like I was failing at everything and it wasn't going to get better. I longed for Heaven, where I wouldn't have to fight to feel happy.

I lifted my gaze up to the sky so that I could take in the view of the mountains and the countryside one more time. Then, across the street, five stories down, I saw a girl from my program running down the sidewalk. She and I had become pretty good friends and we had bonded over how much we missed our friends and families. She ran just about every day and I admired her for that. Somehow that glimpse over the railing, when I was at my lowest, snapped me out of my cloud and I threw myself backward to the safety of a chair. I didn't start crying. I didn't freak out. I wasn't emotional at all. I was barely even thinking as I sat on the balcony and watched my friend disappear from view down the street. God impressed upon me the phrase, "Not today; you're not done yet," and it stuck with me for a while. He still had plans for my life. He did not want me to die that day.

I've never been one to shy away from giving up. If things aren't going the way I want, I'll gladly give up instead of fight and I've never felt guilty about it. Spain was no exception—if you had handed me a plane ticket to the United States at any time in the first half of the semester, I would have taken it and ran, no questions asked. After my experience on that balcony, though, I knew in my gut that I couldn't give up on this, no matter how desperately I wanted to. Many of the other students missed their homes just as much as I, but they remained committed to staying and being part of the community. What right did I have to break that community and repay their investment in me with such a horrible death?

I'd like to tell you that this epiphany marked the end of my depression and that I lived happily ever after. Life in Spain didn't magically get easier once I decided that it was important that I stay. It was still just as difficult to get out of bed the next day. In the end, studying abroad was worth it, but I would not do it all over again. When the program finished, I was overjoyed to come home and get back to the life I had missed so much.

While I really, really hoped that returning home would cure me, it didn't. My moods stayed the same despite the fact that I was back where I felt completely at home.

About a month into my senior year, I attended an evening church service called LOFT (Living Our Faith Together) on campus. I very rarely went to LOFT, but my friend Jessica invited me to go along with her. The theme for that night was "David and Goliath." We read through the story, complete with Pastor Mary's hilarious embellishments, and after that was done, we got down to business: She asked us, point blank, what our giants were. What are the giants that we are afraid to admit to anyone? Struggling in school? Fear? Feeling out of place? Eating disorder? Pornography? Self-doubt? Self-injury? Anxiety? The list goes on. Pastor Mary looked us in the eyes and said, "This giant is not yours to face. This battle doesn't belong to you. David trusted God to deliver him from Goliath, and I want you to trust God to take care of your giant, too. You can trust God. He can do anything. *Anything*. Nothing that you are facing is too big for Him to destroy."

She then invited students to share the giants that they face every day and to claim the power that God has in store for us. One after another, people shared stories of fear, anxiety, depression, eating disorders, identity crises, loneliness, out-of-place-ness, and other things. These brave students publicly (and courageously) shared their giants with us and claimed God's protection, strength, and healing. I was sitting there in awe of their bravery and I knew I would never have the courage to do that in front of all my peers. But as the service came to a close, and the time had passed for me to share, I thought, "Why can't I have that courage? I just need to ask, right? I don't need to be afraid. And even if I am afraid, I don't have to let it consume me. I can stand up and be strong."

That chapel service contributed a great deal to the way that I saw myself and my depression. It helped me realize that I didn't have to be alone in what I was facing. After talking to a few other friends, it suddenly made sense to look into antidepressants. Calvin's counseling center had a psychiatrist come to their offices once a week to meet with students who needed prescriptions. I was a nervous wreck in the waiting room. I had no idea what to expect as I had never visited a therapist's office before. I had never talked to a professional about my feelings. I had never had to take prescription meds every day for any reason. Several times, I felt the urge to escape the waiting room and just blow off the appointment.

The psychiatrist came out to the waiting room and called my name, and I followed him to his office. We sat down, he asked me what brought me to the counseling center that day, and I blurted out, "I want antidepressants, please." The doctor kind of chuckled, and we discussed my symptoms and reasons for deciding to try medication. As we talked, I felt a little bit more comfortable and a little less anxious. He wrote me a prescription for Cymbalta at the end of the appointment and sent me on my way with an appointment in two weeks. He also sent me out with a form to fill out for billing my insurance. Oh, right. I had to pay for this kind of thing, which meant my parents would find out.

I grabbed the bull by the horns and called my dad.

"I went to a doctor today and I'm filling a prescription for an antidepressant," I said.

"Okay," he replied.

"Can you tell Mom?" I asked.

"Uh . . . sure," he said.

End of conversation.

I had a feeling my mom would try to talk me out of it and tell me to get more exercise. I was also afraid that it would somehow get around that I had to be on meds for my mood.

It took a while for me to both physically and cognitively get used to antidepressants. I've been on them now for three years, which is about equal to the amount of time that I struggled with depression before trying medications. Antidepressants don't make my depression go away, but they do help me cope with my symptoms and make it through the day more easily.

Taking antidepressants does not mean that you are weak, or that you've failed, or that you're worthless, or that you're a bad Christian, or anything like that. Making the decision to get treatment for something you can't overcome on your own is actually very strong. I certainly didn't think that way at first, but I've come to think of my pills as little 100-mg doses of God's grace. They clear the fog. They make it easier to focus and get things done, and they help me live my life. I've heard antidepressants roundly denounced by some Christian circles in the name of relying only on God's grace, but why can't God use medicine as an avenue for delivering His grace? Why do we praise God for His miracle of healing through chemotherapy for cancer patients and in the next breath criticize those that take medication for their depression?

Throughout my college years, I struggled not only with depression but also with my identity as a Christian. For so long, I'd heard that Christians don't get depressed and the people who *do* get depressed feel that way because they have turned their backs on God. That's why I initially denied so strenuously that I had depression. I knew I was still a Christian and that I hadn't intentionally turned away from God. If anything, He was the one who had turned away from me because I couldn't hear His voice anymore. I worried that I had done something wrong, that I was continuing to do something wrong without knowing it, and for that reason, I was being punished with depression. I'd never really believed that God punished people for doing bad things, but I couldn't find any other explanation for what was happening.

My story is a counter narrative. Christians can and do suffer from depression. Faith doesn't make you immune. Depression is the result of a chemical imbalance, not sin. If anything, Christians might be *more* susceptible to depression because of the mistaken notion that perfect faith can prevent it. So sadly, many Christians with depression suffer in secret. I avoided telling anyone from my church that I was wrestling with depression because I was afraid of hearing that I needed to recommit my life to Jesus.

We must stop telling our hurting people these lies; they only hurt them more.

There were many times in the past few years that I couldn't feel or hear God at all. My head knew that He was there and always would be, but my heart struggled to believe what my head was saying. I didn't blame God for my depression because I knew (in my head, of course) that God didn't make depression. I struggled to understand why this was all part of God's plan. I thought, "Wouldn't it just be easier to take my depression away? What's the plan here, God? When am I going to be done with this?" It's hard to understand how depression could be part of God's plan if God doesn't want bad things to happen to us. And if He doesn't want bad things to happen to us, then am I outside of God's will in this season of my life? But what about the hairs of my head and the sparrows and nothing happening outside of the will of God? How does this all fit together?

Here's what a year of counseling with a Christian therapist taught me: Depression is neither good nor bad, it just *is*. Having depression doesn't make me a bad person, it doesn't make my parents bad people, it doesn't make me a bad Christian, and it doesn't mean that there is something wrong with me. Life is a series of ups and downs, and depression simply makes the downs seem worse. Depression is part of my life whether I like it or not, but it doesn't have to be bad. It just *is*.

According to the National Institute of Mental Health, depression affects one in fifteen adults at some point in their lives and as many as three in ten college students during any given academic year. That means millions wrestle with depression on a daily basis. The way many Christians view depression is flawed, but I know now that depression doesn't make *me* flawed. It's not a result of sin. It's not my fault. Depression just *is*. That's what I learned in college, but none of that's on my diploma.

QUESTIONS FOR DISCUSSION:

1. How does your faith or nonfaith tradition approach depression? What are the messages (stated or unstated)? How do you interpret Campo's view of her anti-depression medication as "little 100-mg doses of God's grace"?

2. Campo's experience studying abroad was far from the idyllic semester away many colleges advertise. How can colleges and universities address the challenges associated with studying abroad, along with the benefits?

19

THE DATING GAME

God, Ireland, and One Woman of Little Faith

Johnna Purchase

At the top of every college student's resumé should be the title "professional worrier, planner, and list maker." Choice of major, sense of personal vocation, where to live after freshman year, what organization to join or give up, how to divide our weekends between work and play, how to pay for college with work and student loans, whom to date, whether to take Koiné Greek or a nice easy class like World Music. If we can worry about it, as college students, we'll have fussed and fretted over it. Of course, we're sometimes rewarded for all of this worrying as we achieve our goals, but what do we truly gain from all that worrying, planning, and list-making?

For many Christians, our penchant for worrying, planning, and making lists proves a major stumbling block for trusting in God. "Trust. God has a plan for you" often is used to reassure a struggling Christian or as words to celebrate success. Dangerously easy to remember only when things are going well, this phrase, *God's plan*, proves equally suitable as an excuse for sitting back and letting God do all the work (since he has it all figured out). Why should we even bother trying when it will happen his way regardless?

Talking about God's plan remains a murky affair in which the same terms don't mean the same thing to all Christians. One interpretation of what I call "plan theory" posits that every single choice from the significant (like a husband) to the meaningless (like going to a basketball game one random October evening) has been predetermined by God and so we live out this series of choices as our lives. A more moderate interpretation of plan theory insists that God manages only the big decisions of one's life (like whom to marry). Inherent to this discussion of plan theory is the question of God's providence, his caring and acting for good on our behalves. Sometimes, when we say, "God has a plan," we really mean that because God cares about us, he will make sure that events work out for the best, we're talking about God's *providence* rather than God's *plan*.

Based on my ecumenical background having been born into a Baptist church, attending my grandparent's Presbyterian church on holidays, visiting my friend's Lutheran church regularly, attending many of the services and programs my mom directed as the music minister at a Methodist church, visiting my dad's nondenominational church, and volunteering at the church services at my Lutheran college, I understand God's plan as a hybrid between his plan and his providence in which God has planned the big events of my life because he cares for me, he has provided that my life will be good, even if I don't always understand how. Knowing God has a plan without knowing exactly what that plan is sometimes frustrates me more than it heartens me. I find it easy to forget the comfort of God's plan and to worry myself to pieces anyway.

I've especially struggled to trust in God's plan for my young romantic life. A peculiar disconnect occurs in which I firmly trust in God's plan for my future, believing it includes a husband, but I don't readily trust that God's plan also takes care of my meeting that husband. Which doesn't make a lot of sense. Why would God plan a compassionate man for me to spend my life with but leave me stranded to find him? That's like saying God forgot a step. When I or my friends moan, "how will I ever meet someone?" we are implying just that.

Our nervousness about meeting someone remains fairly rational when one considers how the odds seem so greatly stacked against us. My friends and I are committed to dating Christian partners with whom we can share a common understanding of the world and our purpose in it. Consequently, we, like many other young Christians, look for partners within a smaller pool of individuals than the non-Christian population. College provides an excellent opportunity for meeting a wide variety of people with whom we share common interests including our faith—a physics major, the early music singers' ensemble, or the debate team.

This natural pool of potential partners disappears upon graduation. Postgrad, our easy-to-find pool appears limited to the other individuals in our church's young adult group that could be as large as one hundred people or maybe as small as five. Some of them will be dating already and some will not be interested in people of our gender.

We could, of course, meet Christians in the work place, at the gym, while volunteering, or perhaps even through online dating. The tricky part with these alternatives, for me at least, is that unless you're comfortable asking people when you first meet them whether they are Christian or not, it's hard to figure out early on if they are. I'm afraid of meeting a non-Christian and spending emotional and physical energy romantically attaching myself to someone only to find out that I cannot share the most essential part of my life with him. Once again, when I fear this, I'm not fully trusting God.

On top of all of this worry about ever meeting people, we actually have to be interested in one of those Christians we meet. Not all Christians are the same, and the simple fact that someone is a Christian does not make them automatically attractive or even the right person. A person can worry about the odds of finding 1) a Christian, 2) an interesting/similar/suitable/insert-your-criteria individual (college-educated male, if you're like me), and 3) in your small church community. When I realized these odds halfway through my college career, I worried *a lot*.

I waited to date until college. In high school I was too busy studying for AP classes, singing in choir, and acting in plays to give the desired attention to a boyfriend. I also realized I had yet to fully understand myself as a person and so couldn't begin to share myself with another human being. Thinking I was magically all grown up once I got to college, I promptly entered into a relationship. We met through work but only saw each other every Sunday at church. He was a leader in the student congregation council, and I eagerly endorsed the idea of dating a "real Christian." I loved that we'd sit together in daily chapel and on Sundays, feeling as if I were a character in a 1950s book complete with her loving, older, Christian college boyfriend. But, after twelve months of tumultuous dating quite different from my imaginary plot, things ended due to his infidelity.

I entered into a period of self-reflection and discussion with God about why things ended so poorly. I had done my part and found a Christian *leader*. Why did I end up so hurt? I still can't fully answer that question even though I still believe it was part of God's plan for my life, but the question continued to haunt me throughout my sophomore year even as I pined for another brilliant, musical, Christian friend that I ultimately learned wasn't quite as genuine as I had thought.

The summer after my sophomore year, upon watching *500 Days of Summer* and marveling at the disastrous inability of Tom (played by Joseph Gordon-Levitt) to meet someone, I panicked. If the non-Christian characters from the film had so much trouble finding partners when they could date anyone, how would I ever find someone when I only would date Christians? All of the societal and personal pressure I had put off for the past nineteen years, guilt over past "failures," and confusion with God's exact opinion on dating filled me with despair. I temporarily pushed aside my fears after a fitful night of sleep, and summer sped on as I prepared to study for four months at Trinity College in Dublin, Ireland. Focusing on the excitement of moving to a new country (and the worry of not finding housing until after arriving in Dublin) served as a constructive diversion from my dating woes.

While preparing for my trip, friends, coworkers, professors, family, and sometimes even strangers teased me about falling in love with an Irish lad and never coming back to the States. "I have a friend who studied in Denmark and now is married and teaches pre-K in Copenhagen. Don't do that," my roommate would lovingly command me. I responded to the comments by laughing them off and arguing that my interests in Ireland were purely academic; I didn't have time to bother with guys. Dating didn't factor into my plan. I soon learned, however, that God's plan included a quiet, generous young Irishman.

I sat cross-legged on the massive grey steps leading up to the Georgian-era grand dining hall of Trinity College, blue jeans double cuffed a little above the ankle in an attempt to look like the locals. Snuggling into a pullover against the light breeze, I had discarded my shoes in favor of going barefoot (which I later learned undid any attempt to look like a local on a 65-degree, mid-September Wednesday). The Trinity dining hall opens up onto the cobbled front square of Trinity and that week, the week before term began, student societies filled the square with a maze of colorful tables and tents trying to get first year and exchange students to join clubs. The noisy, jumbled scene reminded me of a medieval market. I tried to focus on Flann O'Brien's *At Swim-Two-Birds* while I waited for Christiane to finish meeting with the physics advisor for exchange students so we could go to lunch, but I was hopelessly distracted by an Irish guy that kept running across my line of sight.

I had met the guy a few days before when I signed up to join the Christian Union (CU), and I had struggled to stop thinking about him since. Of average height, slim, with cropped brown hair, glasses, and an exceptionally soft voice, he had only traded a few words with me, but I instantly wanted to be his friend. Today the CU was hosting a free, preterm lunch in a conference room under the dining hall, and he kept running between the CU's table in the square and the lunch under the dining hall. Painfully shy and determined not to bother him, I kept reading.

Much to my relief, I finally noticed a flash of tomato red bobbing toward me. I tried not to smile as I recognized the color of his trousers coming straight for me. "Hey," I tentatively greeted him to which he nervously blurted out, "There's free food that way," pointing for emphasis. After a no less tongue-tied exchange, he left for the lunch. In that moment, I had caught his eye. And, God's plan had once again trumped mine. I finally had spoken with my future partner: Kieran Donoghue.

In the weeks that followed, Kieran and I continued to bump into each other at Thursday night CU meetings, Tuesday lunches with Trinity's chaplains, and in the hallways of the English department. We tried to talk a little more each time. One week I sang as the worship leader and Kieran, the worship coordinator for the CU, played guitar. We talked a little more comfortably by this point, and I entertained the romantic idea of being a Christian-music duo couple. Our mutual interest in the types of worship services sparked an epic e-mail thread that began with YouTube clips of *Holden Evening Vespers* and ended with a request for a first date at a teashop tucked away on a corner of Temple Bar.

Church music finally got us talking, and I reveled in the romantic, Christian nerdiness of it. I imagined telling the story much to the delight and well-timed *awwwws* of family and friends. Our story seemed

to come from a fairy tale, the likes of which a youth pastor would share
with his or her students—

I liked feeling "right."

As the reality of God's gift of Kieran finally sank in, I realized my
silly fantasies about being the poster child example of Christian dating
oversimplified my experience. I could enjoy being in such a picturesque
relationship, but I knew that enjoyment could not provide my sole
source of fulfillment in the relationship or be used as the barometer for
the relationship's health. God would do a lot more in my life through
this relationship than make me a smiling, happy young Christian.

The night we officially began dating, Kieran walked me from a late
evening hymn sing to my bus stop on Dame Street. He waited the
entire twenty-seven minutes with me, and we glowingly, shyly shared
our first impressions of each other. "I prayed a lot about this. I wasn't
quite sure what to do for a while," Kieran admitted softly. My eyes
widened, "Really? Me, too." We broke into grins.

My prayers largely focused on two main points: 1) receiving wisdom
to know how much energy to put into pursuing Kieran, and 2) discernment to know if I should enter into a relationship when, in four months,
I would either have to end it or commit to continuing it from across the
Atlantic. Unfortunately, angels did not visit me during the night nor did
I come across any burning bushes to give me guidance, but I felt a calm
reassurance effectively urging me to relax, trust, and let it be. Trusting
God and letting it be transformed into one of the most positive relation-
ships—romantic or otherwise—in my life.

As the months wore on, Kieran and I continued to learn about one
another. We bonded over our mutual enjoyment of dubstep, but I left
him alone with his Scottish punk bands, and he left me with my operas.
In addition to sharing our faith, we both studied English and loved to
teach each other about our particular areas of interest—Old English
and medieval verse and modernist poetry. We laughed together walking
down the sidewalk as I compulsively smelled the flowers and touched
the moss stubbornly growing amidst the city's concrete and brick, or
excitedly attended a Methodist pastor's fortieth birthday party, mingling
with the other guests in tuxedos and cocktail dresses in happy contrast
with the cozy, tired-looking house. Once flabbergasted that Kieran had
never climbed a tree in his life, I promised to take him climbing at some
point, and he promptly agreed, frankly confessing that he needed more

adventure in his life. And that, among many other things, was what we gave to each other. I opened myself up to the adventure of loving again, and he took the crazy chance of dating someone (an American!) he had just met. Our more quiet temperaments suited each other well, and we traded turns taking the lead, always grabbing the other's hand to pull them into a new adventure. Finally, I had found a Christian man with whom I shared much more in common than our faith.

In a tangible way, our Christianity brought us together. Kieran's nonshowy, purposeful faith wove easily in and out of our lives. When I killed a spider in my flat one afternoon and quipped, "Nobody saw that," he half-jokingly reminded me that "God did." We could easily hop between discussions of the Church as an institution, medieval burial practices, Methodism, men's fashion, evangelism vs. missionary work, and Irish playwrights, without noticing anything odd about it. Many of our weekly social activities centered on church events, but we were just as comfortable spending time walking along the canal or attending a play. Writing out verses to decorate a prayer room, debating the different lenses of literary criticism, and walking around Ovoca Manor at the CU's weekend away, we swapped recipes for favorite childhood desserts. Dating allowed us to fully live in our mutual, Christian world perspectives, sharing a daily Christian background in our conversations while living in a largely secular society. We helped each other grow.

My time in Ireland felt like a modern fairy tale. Every night as I said my prayers, I wholeheartedly thanked God for his amazing provision and generous care. Between my academic courses, new friends, the CU, the city of Dublin itself, and Kieran, I felt the full force of God's love for me. I could only gasp in humbled awe.

The popular saying "all good things must come to an end" may not always be true, but the idea aptly fit my Ireland experience. Against much of my heart's desire, eventually I had to leave Ireland behind, including the university, my new friends, and the man who had captured my heart. Kieran ultimately decided that he could not fully give me the energy a transatlantic relationship required, and we amicably parted, remaining close friends, both still a little hazy about where our affections lie.

My romance abroad makes for a gushy story perhaps familiar to many study abroad participants. It also tells a compelling tale of God providing for one of so little faith. Even now I am dazzled by God's goodness. God gave me a close friend and a glimpse of the beauty and compassions that can be found in a relationship that includes Him. It still strikes me as impossible that I met someone so kind to me with whom our faith provided a focus of service and bond of commonality. I cannot believe this worship-leading, God-lover so stunningly broke from the "contemporary worship" stereotype: a translator of medieval manuscripts, rocking out to dubstep, spending most days in tomato-red trousers, snapping endless candid photographs, performing at poetry slams, and cycling about the larger Dublin area in a neon safety vest. Kieran, just by being himself, complemented my own personality and interests while still teaching me new things and pushing me to grow as a child of God.

Three thousand miles and a foreign culture convinced me I had to trust in God's plan; it's a much better plan than anything I can imagine for myself. I now understand that my glimpses of what God has in store are only that—*glimpses*—and that I won't ever be able to see the whole picture or fully understand how these glimpses fit into the larger whole. I know that God's plan for my vocation, the town I'll live in, my financial security also encompasses a plan for me to meet the man with whom I want to spend the rest of my life. I needn't go after him with a club nor do I need to hurryupandfindhimbeforeIgraduate. Instead, I've learned to trust in the same message God gave me months ago in Ireland: relax, trust, and let it be. This is not always easy to do, especially when I don't even know what God has planned for me tomorrow. But I learned enough from my study abroad to trust God's plan, God's schedule, and God's depthless love for me.

QUESTIONS FOR DISCUSSION:

1. What do you think: Does God have a plan for you?
2. Purchase notes the amazing variety of decisions college students face, many of which can raise anxiety levels. How can students face the reality and import of such decisions without getting overwhelmed with nerves?

20

DEATH AND LIFE

Edward Anderson

Death can make one come alive. In the span of five years, I witnessed the death of my great-grandmothers, grandmother, aunt, uncle, and grandfather. When my grandfather passed away, I discovered the dynamics of life as well as my own significance and purpose.

I was nine years old, and my young notion of compassion, love, and dignity slowly began to fade from my soul. Why me? Why had I been chosen to become a friend to death and witness its bitter sting so often in my short-lived life?

"Your grandfather went to rest in the arms of God last night," my mother said, but my heart went numb as I heard those words. In that moment, I began to doubt the morality of God and the meaning of suffering. Where was God's mercy, love, or justice amidst unexpected death? What kind of God condones inflicting such mental anguish, especially on one so young? In these tragedies, I lost my notion of salvation and deep relationship with humanity, but later, in the philosophies of these departed loved ones and others, I was renewed.

My father and mother raised me in a middle class, African American, Christian home twenty minutes outside the urban core of Atlanta. My father, a man not of formal education, but a veteran of the military and a minister, instilled in me from a young age the value of serving others in need. These teachings were based upon his scriptural understanding of what God requires from "his" children. Equally important, my father imprinted on me to be the "head and not the tail." By this he meant we should do everything we're capable of to be the best without compromising morals and character. My father's notion is rooted in Pauline doctrine of the New Testament and, therefore, is viewed as a mandate of God.

My father's theology could be summarized as 1) God is the same yesterday, today, and forever; and 2) you must stand on God's word while being true to the identity God has created for you (Hebrews 13:8). But, I cannot reconcile this theological understanding with my experiences of God. My father understands God as rigid, codified, and unchanging throughout time—all-powerful with a "divine plan" to which we must adjust. My father's God tends to be paternalistic and unmoving—a noun—while my experiences have taught me that God is a verb; God dwells *with us*.

My late grandfather, the Revered Willie Anderson Sr., left an indelible impression upon my perspective of the world. My lifelong dream of becoming an agent of positive change in my community started with him and was fostered by my father's preaching and ministerial activities. My grandfather grew up poor and poorly educated in Liberty County, Georgia, but that did not stop him from becoming County Commissioner and speaking up for his poor neighbors who otherwise would not have had a voice in politics or policy.

While the lessons of my father and grandfather were ingrained in my theological foundations of God, to me they were actually not about God Godself. My father and grandfather gave me a conception of God as they knew "him," of a God that was confined to Scripture and acted out of a tough love. This became apparent when I found myself peering at the lifeless body of my grandfather and posing the question, "If God is love and all-powerful, why cause so much pain and suffering?"

I was certain that my grandfather, grandmothers, and uncle had all died unjustly. They were the embodiment of love. If I'm honest with myself, these moments of questioning, moments when my lived experience challenged my family's teachings on the authority of Scripture, brought my search for faith and meaning to an impasse. Life had gotten in the way of how I was taught to understand Scripture. My family's African American faith tradition was important to my identity. In it the Christian faith is restless, free, and brimming with hope. But my thoughts outside the tradition left me feeling isolated. I questioned the doctrine of the churches where my father preached. I remained deeply committed to the *practice* of faith, but highly skeptical of its connection to the holy text.

When I entered Morehouse College, I gained language—and wisdom—to encounter these challenges, and wrestle with them anew. I quickly found works of the theologian Howard Thurman, such as *The Search for Common Ground* and *Jesus and the Disinherited*, essential to my journey. It was Thurman who once explained to Gil Bailie: "Don't ask yourself what the world needs. Ask yourself what makes you come alive and then go do that. Because what the world needs is people who have come alive."[1] With the death of my family members who were the foundation for my values and morality, grew an understanding that selflessness and humility are essential to human flourishing. These two revelations accompanied another personal quest: the need for me to shatter the glass box of what had developed into a strong inferiority complex, glass walls that had grown increasingly thick as I struggled to find my own path amidst my theological frustrations with my family.

In this tension between being a preacher's kid, loving my father and his preaching but also questioning it, and gleaning from theological study in college, I was able to carve out a place for God that dealt with my inferiority complex. My new understanding of the fabric of God was woven together by the theological underpinnings of the African American experience of the soul and ancestors. For me, understanding the soul allowed me to interpret God as energy that in turn renders us as finite energy incarnate. The paradox of free will became unraveled by the words of Howard Thurman, and my new discoveries deepened by studying Ralph Waldo Emerson and the theologian Paul Tillich. Through the use of reason and by embracing my internal struggles, my inferiority eventually gave way to a more genuine self. Prayer became nothing more than thoughts and drawing closer to the ultimate reality, and my soul was emboldened with the courage to be.

During the summer after my freshman year, I served in AmeriCorps under the Volunteers In Service to America (VISTA) program with the Morehouse College Community Revitalization Initiative. The focus of the program is the economic development through revitalization of the

---

1. Gil Bailie attributes this quote to Howard Thurman in the forward of Bailie's book *Violence Unveiled* (New York: Crossroad Publishing, 1995) xv.

West End Atlanta area, one of the poorest minority-concentrated areas in Atlanta, and surrounding community. As a student of Morehouse College, it was not often that I had the opportunity to engage with the residents of the West End Atlanta area on a personal level, void of stigmas and false perceptions. It was through my AmeriCorps service, community meetings, and walking through neighborhoods that a stronger love for the community, as well as the need to inspire hope within others grew within me. Learning about the issues that plagued the community presently, and the historical fabric of the neighborhoods, motivated me each day to make efforts to bring hope once again to the West End.

Walking through the neighborhoods in the West End caused a new rush of concerns about suffering in the world. The people with whom I interacted were of the same race as me, but from totally different cultural and economic realities. I recognized my privilege. Previously, I had only interacted with African Americans in this part of Atlanta as a work of charity rather than passion. That summer of service, impacting the lives of residents, transformed my interactions with the community into a feeling of connection to the very essence of God. Bringing hope to a community that once thrived with possibility was an extension of God *with us*, a God that felt the pain, confusion, and suffering of the people rather than being removed from it. These experiences taught me that, at its best, service to others helps remind us of the humanity in every man, woman, or child.

I experienced my new understanding of God in an encounter I had with a young boy in the West End named Travis. The sun was beaming upon the worn asphalt as my colleague and I conducted a land inventory in Cascade. As we took in the condition of the property and assessed the possible needs, we heard a whistling noise behind us. When we turned around, we found a young boy around the age of nine on a bike pedaling briskly toward us. As he came closer, we noticed that he was trying to kick us from his bike in an attempt to expel us from his neighborhood. Suddenly, he stopped and asked, "Who do you work for, the government?" Confused, I asked the boy his name and he reluctantly said Travis. I asked him why he was trying to kick us, since we did not know each other. Travis told me that I did not belong there and that I was an outsider, and he did not trust outsiders. As Travis continued to talk to me, a solemn feeling came over me for Travis felt that people did not care if he succeeded or not. He felt as if people did not care about him or his neighborhood and that we were there to kick his family out of his hood, the only home he had ever known. Travis went on to tell me that he had dreams and wanted to own his own business, but that he did not know how. After listening to Travis and inviting him to accept me as friend, not a foe, my framework for God shifted again.

From talking to Travis and visiting his reality for those brief moments, my understanding of *God with us* changed significantly. In some ways, Travis was me. He was a black boy in America. He had to deal with feelings of inadequacy just as I did. But Travis was different than me. Travis was willing to protect the only family, the only neighborhood, the only people he knew that cared for him, and he was willing to go against two older guys to prove it. Travis was willing to defend the only manifestations of God, of love, of faith that he knew. In a way, Travis represented the best and worst of my upbringing. He reminded me of the isolation I felt as child, but Travis also helped me realize the benefits of faith in oneself and one's community.

I no longer understand God as the author of my life with a predefined end, but as an editor and companion of the journey-incarnate life. One summer day in Atlanta, in a place very different from West End, I heard a lecture by Dr. Monica Coleman on process theology. Coleman shared how she understands God, a God who both allowed and suffered with her through depression. After the talk, Dr. Coleman gave me a copy of her book, *Making a Way Out of No Way*. In the front pages she wrote, "Edward, find your own theological voice" and I felt freed to embrace my new understandings of God. I have come to claim a more mystical Christianity, opening my mind to one of the highest realizations of God in the world, Jesus. To do so, I've had to reconcile my understanding of Jesus as taught to me as a child with my new worldview.

In the summer of 2012, I was invited to attend an interreligious education conference with two of my Morehouse brothers and chapel assistants, Rashad and Segun. The conference took place at a Jewish retreat center in the rural forest of Connecticut. During the first night of the conference, a Jewish friend of Rashad and Segun invited us to participate and observe a Jewish prayer service, held so someone could say *Kaddish*, the prayer said by mourners of the deceased. Slowly, men and women began to assemble in the room until ten were present. Then at once they begin to chant in Hebrew the prayer of remembrance. Watching the men and women rocking back and forth with prayer books in hand and heads bowed in deep reverence displayed for me the love of the community. The Jewish individuals did not know each other, but they still gathered together in remembrance of their departed. Once more, as I watched the melodic rocking back and forth, my faith became more fully reconciled. I saw how death was brought together in love, hope, and active engagement of the community. I witnessed how another's grief gave strength.

My college faith journey has been full of discovery. My upbringing in my family's church supported a deep faith, but one that I needed to question and make my own. I have not traveled alone, but with Howard Thurman and Travis, Dr. Coleman, Morehouse brothers, and Jewish conferees. I have come to believe that God is loving and caring for all of humanity—that even at our lowest moments, God is with us. When we cannot see it, we must look harder, for God is always present, even and especially in the love of those we encounter on the way.

QUESTIONS FOR DISCUSSION

1. How has your family's faith affected your own?
2. For Anderson, the experience of serving neighbors off campus was significant in his journey. How can colleges better support community service and thoughtful reflection on it?

21

STRANGE BENEDICTION

Joseph Paillé

"Not like that. Do you know any praise songs?"

"What's a praise song?"

It is an unusually cold night for early June in Gardiner, Montana. I arrived in Gardiner that afternoon for a summer of Christian ministry in Yellowstone National Park. Since making the trek down Route 89 from Bozeman to Mammoth Hot Springs, my day has been a blur of paperwork, introductions, and what my ministry team refers to as "call stories." After eating cheeseburgers from the grill at a local churchgoer's home, we drift from his shag-carpeted living room to the backyard fire pit. As the sun slouches behind Mt. Everts, the sky becomes filled with so many stars that my attempt to identify constellations is overtaken by a sheer sense of awe. Could it be that this is even a sense of what the others around the campfire call, "God's presence"? Or am I projecting something toward the night sky?

I am snapped back to the campfire by a request. "Joe! Go get your guitar and play us a song." I would normally be hesitant to sing for other people but, moved by a new sense of adventure, I oblige. As I stumble through the backyard to get my guitar from the house, I decide to play Sam Cooke's "Wonderful World," a song my father often sang to me when I was little. As I begin to strum the chords, I'm surprised to find my normally flat voice to be more pliant than usual. The cold hasn't left my fingers stiff and lethargic either. My enthusiasm evaporates, however, as I finish the last "what a wonderful world this would be" and look up to half a dozen confused faces.

When I moved to Minnesota to go to college, I was what most people would call a "lapsed Catholic." I'd gone to Catholic school for most of my life, but didn't have a lot of interest in organized religion anymore. The only time I attended a church service my first semester of college was during Family Weekend. I didn't have anything against religion, but didn't feel a strong attraction to it either. It was a nice thing for other people, just not for me.

The spring of my first year, I enrolled in a class on non-Western biblical interpretation to fulfill the required religion credit for first-year students. That my professor was a white Protestant woman who assigned works by authors from Asia, Latin America, and Africa intrigued me, but it was what I learned about my own faith that kept me interested in the course. Since the syllabus covered the entire Bible, one of the first readings we did in the course was on the tower of Babel from Genesis 11. In the story, humans build a megalopolis with a giant brick tower tall enough to reach into the heavens, but fail when God confounds their speech and scatters them across the earth. What struck me about the reading was not its discussion of the origins of language or what the story had to say about human potential, but the more basic question of whether God was up above humanity. All of my life, I had heard about prayers being "offered up to God" or how Jesus "came down from heaven." When I was younger, the notion that God was above me seemed somewhat odd, as if I could breach the ontological divide when I flew on an airplane. Yet I still assumed that this was the way good Christians thought about God. Was that not right? Were there Christians who didn't think that? And if God didn't hover above humanity, what else didn't I know?

As we worked through the syllabus, I realized that I never really asked questions about the Bible or God while I was in Catholic school. I remember feeling frustrated when one of my middle school classmates asked how Jesus was raised from the dead and was told, "It's a mystery of our faith." It felt constricting, as if I could ask questions I knew the answers to but not the ones we really cared about, such as why people who were nice still got sick, or if kids would ever stop picking on me because of my leg braces. And so faith never really became personal for me. I knew some of the Bible stories and could follow along during mass, but I never understood much of what I was doing or what it might have to do with my life. Almost a decade later, as the Minnesota winter strained to turn into spring, I began to realize that there were other ways of thinking about beliefs.

There's a somewhat cliché saying among youth pastors and concerned parents that college students will "lose their faith" when they study religion in college, as if faith is something that can only be eroded away over time. There is no shortage of advice telling parents to build up their child's faith in high school and just try to minimize the inevitable damage that will come in the college seminars. But the exposure to critical readings of the Bible, such as questioning the idea of God as up above, was something of a revelation to me. It was like overhearing a conversation I wanted to be a part of just as I was getting ready to leave the room.

Later that spring, I was walking to dinner with a friend one night after track practice when I glanced at a handwritten sign—Summer Job Fair: Black and Gold Ballrooms. I didn't have any plans for the summer and thought I might find a job in town, so I told my friend I'd catch up and shuffled over to the job fair. As I walked through the display tables of summer camps, volunteer programs, and corporate internships, I picked up brochures and made polite small talk, but refrained from taking any applications. Finally, as my stomach growled, at the end of the room I came to a display for a summer ministry program in the national parks. I mentioned to the recruiter that I was sure my uncle had done something like this once in the 1970s and that my mom's college roommate's son did a similar thing once, but I really couldn't remember. As I stammered through my introduction, it occurred to me that this could be my chance to find out what I thought about my faith. There were only a few weeks left of the religion class and I was seeking some way to keep discerning my own beliefs. Participating in a ministry was unlike anything I'd ever done. But if nothing else, I hoped it would give me the time and space to figure out my own beliefs. I had declared myself an economics major earlier that fall, putting myself on track for summer internships after sophomore and junior years and a career as an entry-level demand analyst after graduation. I thought I could afford to take a summer to get my faith figured out and then go back to focusing on economics. After scarfing down dinner with the track team, I jogged over to the library and started filling out my application.

It's been two days since my introduction to praise music. My ministry team and I are sitting around a minuscule coffee table in the family room of Mammoth's hotel. The mural of bison on the wall overlooks a room strewn with half-completed puzzles and unfolded maps of the park. That weekend, our ministry team will host our first worship service in one of the village campgrounds. Brian, a scruffy surfer from California, has taken the lead on assigning pieces from the suggested order of service: Call to Worship, Opening Prayer, Legal Disclaimer (to be read during the offering), Gospel Reading. The pieces are snatched up as soon as Brian announces them. But there's one part of the service no one wants to take: Preaching.

The other members of my ministry team express their desire to share the Gospel with campers while bemoaning their fear of public speaking. I, on the other hand, enjoy public speaking, but can't comprehend getting up in front of people to talk about what the Bible might have to say about their lives. The conversation moves from awkward silence, to earnest encouragement, to sarcastic jabbing back, to awkward silence. I move my gaze away from the table to the maps around the room and it occurs to me. "I'll do it." All eyes are now on me. "Alright, Joe!" says Brian, his bandana-wrapped head nodding up and down. There are a few pats on the back and a thumbs up from the local pastor who happens to walk through the room.

That night I pick up the *HarperCollins Study Bible* that I bought for my first-year religion class and flip through the Old Testament trying to find something to preach on. Since meeting the other members of the ministry team, I have noticed that my Bible looks a little too new, lacking the dog-eared pages and colorful border of sticky notes that my team members' Bibles have. As I look for texts to preach on, I highlight passages and write *Exactly!* in the margin, hoping to make my Bible blend in better with the rest of the team's. As I scan the index, I begin to second-guess coming to Yellowstone. It was a crazy idea, traveling a thousand miles to do ministry with a group of people I'd never met before whose beliefs I didn't really share. I didn't know what I thought about the Bible or God, let alone Jesus. I didn't have a favorite Bible verse or know any praise songs. Worst of all, my call story, which normally serves as one's calling card into Christian circles, was less than thirty seconds long.

Mulling over that conversation I had with the recruiter at the job fair, I set out for a walk around the hot springs to clear my mind and get some fresh air. The hot springs in Mammoth are surrounded by board-walks that go up toward Bunsen Peak, named after the man who invented the Bunsen burner found in high school chemistry labs. The hot springs look like something from a science fiction movie, sulfuric smoke covering the strange array of colors that lie under the surface of the water. Standing on the boardwalk over one of the pools, I think back to a story we read in my first-year religion class, something about water coming from rocks. As soon as I recall the story, my mind floods with possible illustrations for the sermon. Renewed with possibility, I ramble back down the boardwalk toward my room and flip through my Bible to find the passage. Exodus 17:1–7. I have a text.

Three weeks later, I drive to the amphitheater in the nearby Tower campground, ready to preach on Rahab's story from Joshua 2. After-ward, a man with a thick mustache and cowboy hat approaches me and says, "I'd love to be in your church after you become a pastor." I laugh the suggestion off in my head. Well, I can't do that, obviously, because I'm not really religious. All I can manage is a smile and a weak, "Yeah, who knows. Maybe one day."

Though the act of preaching has become more comfortable, I'm still struggling with how to manage and present my personal beliefs. I find myself especially confused about the nature of Jesus and why God isn't sufficient. Though I have received positive feedback on my preaching, no one has questioned why I haven't preached from the Gospels yet, as all the other team members. I feel like an impostor, waiting to be found out.

When I raise my questions at one of the ministry team's devotional Bible studies, it quickly becomes clear that we can hardly communicate. I hear phrases like "died for your sins" and "so you can have eternal life," but they feel foreign, as if they are from another language. They feel like answers to questions that I am not asking. I recognize all the words, but they don't connect with anything else I know or have experienced. I express some of the same concern in phone calls and letters with friends, but their emotional support can't really help me sort out my theological problems. I feel stuck. I'm told that I'm good at what I'm doing, maybe even called by God to be doing, but I'm not sure I should be doing it.

Though my beliefs are still cloudy, by late July I find myself trying on more and more of my ministry team's language and habits. Though I still have my doubts, I hope that by putting on the evangelical language and ethos, my theological beliefs will sort themselves out as well. In the journal I've been keeping all summer, I scribble phrases like, "Felt God's presence today," or "Great afternoon to experience God." I work to stretch my call story to a whole two minutes. When I am invited up to sing a praise song with the other team members one Sunday, it doesn't feel wholly uncomfortable. Even though I don't know the words, the song is repetitive enough that I can figure out the bridge and chorus fairly easily.

One night as I am getting off my shift at the gas station, I run into my ministry supervisor who asks me if I can preach in the larger chapel that coming Sunday. "Yeah, sure," I respond. "Where are you guys headed?" expecting they are headed to Bozeman or Billings for the weekend. He looks confused for a second before his head jerks back in a moment of recognition. "Oh, nowhere. I've heard really good things about your preaching and I just want to give you a chance to preach in the big chapel. I'll be there." I take him up on the offer and preach there the next weekend. After the service, I do the usual shaking of hands and small talk. People seemed to have gotten something out of the sermon, and I'm relieved not to have made any Freudian slips. A man approaches me and asks if he can pray for me. I accept, thinking he'll act like the bushy-mustached man, just say a few kind words and throw on an *Amen* at the end. Instead, he puts his hand on my head, thanks the Lord Jesus for my proclamation of the Word, and prays for what feels like five minutes.

Though I thanked the man for his prayer and told him to have a blessed weekend, the experience shakes me. For someone who thought of praying as mumbling through the rosary or adoring the Blessed Sacrament, the physical intensity of his prayer hit something deep within me. In my first-year religion class, I had been able to play with theological ideas while always keeping them at arm's length. I could write a paper about an author's argument without having to put my own beliefs at stake. Even when I preached in Yellowstone I often felt like I was preaching another person's faith but as long as people told me how good of a job I was doing I figured I was making good progress. But as the man moved his hand toward my forehead, it felt like he was pushing all the doubts, questions, and uncertainty back on to me. I knew that I couldn't hold my faith at arm's length anymore.

It was around this time that I went off of my antidepressants. I'd been taking them for a little over a year, since the spring of my senior year of high school when I began having feelings of guilt and unworthiness for no apparent reason. I was one of the top students in my class, a leader of a community service organization, a varsity cross country runner, and had gotten into most of the colleges I'd applied to. But I felt driven more by a feeling of failure than a desire to succeed. When I received a fat envelope from Kenyon College, I felt not joy but a pang of dread about what might happen if I went there. After a few sessions with a therapist I realized that the feelings I was having stemmed from worry about not achieving enough and letting people down. For the first time in my life I could choose where I lived, what I studied, and where I worked. But instead of grasping the opportunity, I was terrified of making the wrong choice. The anxiety got worse and the depression, which I was hoping was some kind of seasonal affective disorder that would go away on its own, didn't let up. My parents, the therapist, and I decided it would be best if I stayed on a low dosage of medication during my first year of college.

On one of my last weekends in the park, a team member and I went for a hike along a plateau on the western side of the park. We'd become good friends over the summer while running services together but hadn't spent much time talking about our personal beliefs. On the way back to the car, she talked about how she liked hiking because it gave her time to talk with God, not in a vaguely spiritual kind of way but in deeply personal conversation. I told her that I appreciated how open she was about her faith and the conversation moved on.

One of the things that stuck with me most that summer was how my team members talked about God's involvement in their lives. They saw God acting in their lives in myriad ways every day, guiding decisions, keeping them company, and hearing their prayers. But most importantly, their lives taught them about God. After that hike, I began to realize that the God I had started questioning was not only "up" in a directional sense but an emotional one as well, something of an absentee landlord for my life. I had thought of faith as a predetermined set of ideas and practices that existed independent from my own life. But as I thought back on my own experience with anxiety, I came to wonder if it too might have something to tell me about God.

All summer I had been avoiding the Gospels. Phrases like "died for your sins" and "so you can have eternal life" hadn't meant anything to me because they didn't relate to my life. I was depressed because I was so worried about letting people down. I didn't need to hear anything more about my sinfulness. And I didn't think much about eternal life because I was just trying to figure out the one I was living. For the first time, I read not to write a paper or to clarify some idea, but to see whether my life might help me sort out my beliefs. As I read I began to see that in the Gospels God is not removed from the people but deeply intertwined in their lives. What I found was not a God who was ambivalent about my life, but a God who cared so much about people like me that God lived among them. Jesus counseled them about their hurts and their struggles, talked with them about their dreams and their hopes for the future. And I began to see that the times when my depression was the worst were the times when I took it upon myself to achieve a kind of perfection in my life. But what I needed wasn't a perfect life, but permission to have flaws.

On my last night in Yellowstone, I went to the gas station where I worked that summer to say goodbye. August was sliding away and there was a slight chill in the air again, much like my first night at the park. In grass across from the gas station, a herd of elk wandered around while tourists tracked them with their cameras. And as the shadows of the gas pumps grew longer on the concrete I began to think about everything that had happened that summer. I thought about the first Sunday I preached, the praise songs I hadn't learned, and how I almost skipped the job fair so I could get back to studying sooner. But I thought most about the man's hand on my forehead. What I thought was a prayer turned out to be an unexpected and strange benediction for the summer. I had gone to Yellowstone to try to figure out my beliefs, to get them straightened out so I could get back to what I was supposed to be doing.

As my plane took off from the Bozeman airport the next morning, I knew that I was never going to have it all figured out. But I was still going in peace.

QUESTIONS FOR DISCUSSION:

1. Paillé notes that he sometimes encountered, "answers to questions that I am not asking" during his summer at Yellowstone. What experiences does this phrase suggest for you?

2. Writer Diana Butler Bass suggests that Christian belief today comes in this order: *belonging* to a community, then *behaving* similarly to that community, and then *believing* the faith of the community. How do you see this progression in Paillé's essay? How do you experience belonging, behaving, and belief in your own life?

3. For many college students, the summer allows for a time of faith-filled reflection and discovery. This is certainly the case for Paillé, though he mentions at several points how his summer built on his religious study in the college classroom. How can colleges and universities better connect students' summer experiences to the classroom?

ABOUT THE CONTRIBUTORS

Edward Anderson is a native of Atlanta, Georgia, and a 2012 cum laude graduate of Morehouse College with a Bachelors of Arts in Political Science. Currently, he is a Master of Comparative Religion student at Claremont School of Theology. As a community organizer, grant writer, and public speaker, he seeks to be an agent for social justice and a pluralistic society.

Taylor Brorby served as the 2013–2014 writer-in-residence at Holden Village, a Lutheran retreat center in North Central Washington. He reviews books for the *Englewood Review of Books*, is a contributing editor for *The EcoTheo Review*, and blogs for *The Huffington Post*. Taylor has received grants from St. Olaf College, Hamline University, and the North Dakota Humanities Council. His essays have appeared in numerous publications, among them the *Northern Plains Ethics Journal*, *Orion*, numerous newspapers, and Augsburg Fortress Press. He is working on a vespers service for climate change and speaks regularly at colleges about fracking and environmentalism.

Andrew Leigh/Amanda LeAnn Bullard, blessed with a complex network of identities, has a Masters in Library Science and a BS in Crime and Delinquency Studies and Information Resource Studies. With a constant drive to serve others, they have worked in prison and academic libraries, churches, camps, and a police department. To rest they enjoy crafting, reading, hiking, and medieval recreation. They currently engage in vocational discernment with the Episcopal Service Corps and look forward to the path ahead.

Andrea Campo is a graduate of Calvin College in Grand Rapids, Michigan, and is currently working on a Master's degree in school counseling at Western Michigan University. When she isn't working or studying, Andrea reads voraciously and hopes someday to be an advocate for students affected by mental illness. You can find more of her writing at http://longingfortheheavenlycountry.blogspot.com.

Allison Chubb is an ordained Anglican priest and works as a college chaplain and parish outreach coordinator. She has a passion for reimagining church by living at the intersection of the ancient and the future, using our inherited faith to engage a generation of postmodern questions. When she isn't priesting, Allison can be found in her garden, beading, or creating art. She lives in Winnipeg, Manitoba with her cat, Chai.

Kristi Del Vecchio is a 2013 graduate of Concordia College in Moorhead, Minnesota, where she studied biology and religion. During her time at Concordia, however, she tried not to let school get in the way of learning. She spent her time organizing the Better Together Interfaith Alliance, planning service projects, enjoying live music, and drinking too much coffee. Today Kristi is an Associate on the Operations team at Interfaith Youth Core in Chicago, Illinois, where her interest in interfaith cooperation, live music, and coffee continues to be satiated.

Anna DeWeese earned her MA in Systematic Theology from Union Theological Seminary in New York City where her work focused on interfaith and intra-Christian dialogue, and Christian social justice. She earned her BA in Religion from Hendrix College in Conway, Arkansas. Currently, she works for the CARE for Teachers program, a mindfulness-based professional development program for educators, and she teaches for the Interfaith Community, Inc. to provide religious education to Jewish-Christian families. She also serves as a national board member to Church Women United, Inc., and was previously a contributing scholar to the *Journal for Inter-Religious Dialogue's* blog "State of Formation."

Lydia Hawkins hails from the small, Midwestern town of Tipton, Indiana, where the stoplights are sparse and the pizza joints plenty. She is a 2014 graduate of Valparaiso University, completing her studies in psychology, theology, and Spanish. Frequenting coffee shops, the great outdoors, and places of worship, Lydia is often found barefoot and pensive. She most enjoys spending time with family and friends, gardening, trying new recipes, and reading and writing. When she grows up, she hopes to be more loving.

Mary Ellen "Jem" Jebbia is a Master of Divinity student at the University of Chicago studying interfaith and Islam in the United States. Jem self-identifies as a Mahayana Buddhist and serves as a member of the Spiritual Life Council at the University of Chicago. In the past, she has written for *The Huffington Post*, the *Journal for Inter-Religious Dialogue's* blog "State of Formation," and the Interfaith Youth Core's blog. After graduating, Jem hopes to work in the interfaith youth movement and to train young interfaith leaders.

Michelle Johnson holds a bachelors degree in History, Spanish, and Chican@ and Latin@ Studies from the University of Wisconsin-Madison. She has moved back to the Minneapolis–St. Paul area in Minnesota, where she is re-rooting herself in family and place while exploring her interests in local and sustainable food systems, herbalism, and other holistic forms of personal and communal health and healing.

Hillary Martinez lives in Berkeley, California as she works toward completing a Master of Arts in Systematic and Philosophical Theology at Graduate Theological Union. She received her Bachelor's degree in English from Duke University and hopes to continue pursuing her love of literature and writing as an English teacher at the high school level. Hillary is immensely grateful for the friendship and support of the Duke Chapel PathWays program at Duke University, which has played an indispensable role in fostering her love of theology and in walking with her as she grows in her understanding of vocational discernment.

Joseph Paillé is a candidate for ordained ministry in the Evangelical Lutheran Church in America. A graduate of Princeton Theological

Seminary and St. Olaf College, Joseph has worked with Augsburg Fortress, the Lutheran Coalition for Public Policy in Minnesota, A Christian Ministry in the National Parks, and numerous congregations. He
lives in New York City with his wife, Anna.

Steven Porter completed his undergraduate studies in 2012 at Indiana
Wesleyan University, where he studied media communication and jour-
nalism as a member of the Mary C. Dodd Honors Program. He was
raised in a Pentecostal church but has since found a greater sense of
belonging in the mainline tradition. He's pursuing a career in journal-
ism and hopes his work will foster civic engagement.

Agnes Potamian, armed with a BA degree, curiosity, and a beat-up car,
is not-so-gracefully learning to navigate the proverbial "real world." She
is still pursuing a life and career in ministry with the Episcopal Church.
Like all good millennials, she is subsisting on coffee, $4 wine, and her
iPhone.

Johnna Purchase, a senior English major at St. Olaf College, spends her
days in the library researching modernist literature, especially World
War I poetry and James Joyce's *Ulysses*. At school she serves as the
Community Outreach Coordinator for the Student Congregation
Council and as a weekly Communion assistant. A regular bookworm,
Johnna spends her summers and breaks working in rare book libraries.
When not in a library, she spends her free time singing in choir, dream-
ing about travel, writing short stories, running outside with her room-
mate, reading baking blogs, and laughing with friends.

Rick Reiten is a pastor currently serving at Bristol Lutheran in Sun
Prairie, Wisconsin. Ministry opportunities have taken him to Columbia,
South Carolina, and Moorhead, Minnesota, as well. He spends time
running, refinishing wood furniture, gardening, traveling, watching sunsets, and drinking good wine with his wife, Lindsay. Together as partners, they experience the joys and challenges of life, including how to
parent their three-year-old daughter Anya. He appreciates all the
friends, family, and mentors who have shaped him along the way.

Brandan Robertson is a writer, speaker, activist, and the dreamer behind the Revangelical Movement that seeks to rethink, reform, and
renew Evangelical Christian faith for a new age. He received his BA in
Pastoral Ministry and Theology from Moody Bible Institute in Chicago.
He is also a writer for *Red Letter Christians, Sojourners* "God's Politics"
blog, and a number of other online sources. Brandan currently resides
in Washington, D.C.

Lauren Deidra Sawyer received her Master of Arts in Theology and
Culture at the Seattle School of Theology and Psychology, where she
wrote her thesis on John Updike, St. Augustine, and the canonization of
erotic saints. She currently lives in Seattle with her beloved, signed
copy of Updike's *Rabbit, Run*. Learn more about Lauren at laurendei-
dra.com.

Kyle Thorson received a bachelor's degree in political science from the
University of North Dakota in 2011. Following graduation, he volunteered for a year with an organization that advocates for drug war victims in Cuernavaca, Mexico, and learned about immigration and social
justice issues between the United States and Mexico. Closer to home,
Kyle played an integral role crafting and passing a city ordinance making Grand Forks the first North Dakota city to provide discrimination
protections for sexual orientation and gender identity in housing and
public employment. He continues to be active in his faith community as
he pursues a master's degree in public administration.

Br. Lawrence A. Whitney, LC+ serves as University Chaplain for Community Life at Boston University's Marsh Chapel. He is a professed
member and priest in the Lindisfarne Community, an ecumenical neo-
monastic religious order based in Ithaca, New York. Br. Larry is completing his PhD in philosophical theology at the Boston University
School of Theology.

Michael Casey W. Woolf is an American Baptist pastor serving as associate pastor for youth and children at First Baptist Church in Lexington,
Massachusetts. Michael holds a Master of Divinity from Harvard Divinity School where he is studying toward a Doctor of Theology.

Kissing in the chapel,
 praying in the frat house